EDUCATING
for HUMAN
GREATNESS

AN EXPANDED SECOND EDITION

Lynn Stoddard

with Anthony Dallmann-Jones
and Other Extraordinary Educators

the Peppertree Press
Sarasota, Florida

For information regarding permission,
call 941-922-2662 or contact us at our website:
www.peppertreepublishing.com or write to:
the Peppertree Press, LLC.
Attention: Publisher
1269 First Street, Suite 7
Sarasota, Florida 34236

ISBN: 978-1-936051-83-0

Library of Congress Number: 2010920923

Printed in the U.S.A.

Printed April 2010

This book is first dedicated to my favorite teachers:
My lovely wife, our 12 beautiful children and
their strong spouses, and my 84+ grandchildren.

❦

I especially wish to dedicate this book
to all of the extraordinary teachers
who are trying to keep their heads above water
while swimming against the strong current
of top-down false reforms.

PROLOGUE
ON BEING AMAZED

I like being amazed. I love the sense of wonder that comes over us when we are intrigued by something—fully alert for each little piece of new information, followed by an overwhelming sense of curiosity to know more, and more, and more. If you had/have a hobby that you love, you know about the "I want to know more!" feeling—to explore and dig out every scrap of information you can about something that is fascinating to you.

Have you seen a little baby looking over its Mom's shoulder at the world? A little bobble-headed human, eyes wide, mouth open, trying to hold its head erect to see more. Inside, it must be experiencing genuine amazement and, without knowing the words, saying to itself, "What is that?!" And, "HEY! What is THAT!?!?!" Hey, look over THERE!" I have a friend who told me about his infant son who woke up in his crib one bright sunshiny morning, stood up, holding to the rail, looked out the window and exclaimed with eyes wide open, "WOW!"

This "amazement factor" in every baby is a natural part of being human. Maslow located the "The Need to Know" in the *growth needs* area, way above the physiological needs, the survival needs, the status needs, the affection needs. *The Need to Know* is right up there with the pinnacle needs of *The Need to Create* and the holy grail of human development: *The Need for Self-Actualizing*. Yes, *The Need to Know* is one of the highest in the hierarchy of human needs. "But wait," you say, "I thought those higher needs were reserved for mature, wise adults. You are saying that babies can be at the *top* of the hierarchy?"

Yes! It is a large part of the baby's natural state of being! In actuality, the child is consumed by *The Need to Know*. When not hungry, or otherwise uncomfortable, children are relentless in expressing their need to know things. That is pretty much all they want to do: "Let me at it! I want to explore *that*!"

What a natural, wonderful hunger is *The Need to Know*. It begins in children but, unfortunately, is often killed by the thing we call *school*. Children naturally want to learn more and more, but at some point—you may not remember when—you began to want to know less and less of what teachers were trying to teach you. As a professor of undergraduates for many years, I cannot count the times I basically heard, "Just tell us what you want." In other words, learning has become a laborious obstacle course to navigate in order to gain, in and of itself, a worthless thing called a *grade*.

So, we begin life with: "I want to KNOW!" In healthy children, you will see that same eagerness in them as they troop off to kindergarten. Perhaps not in kindergarten, but certainly soon thereafter, *The Need to Know* is replaced by a thing called *learning* and it is a series of *tasks*. Suddenly it is known as *work*—desk *work*, home *work*, finish your *work*, hand in your *work*, and teachers write on your papers, *"Nice work!"*, and tell you to *work* hard and you will get something special because everyone knows that you get paid for *work* because *work* means something unpleasant—something you do not want to do. You do it only because you are threatened or bribed to do it. It is no longer natural. It is no longer fascinating. It is no longer amazing.

By the time children reach high school much of their studying and learning is directed toward trying to outguess the teacher or test makers in order to NOT get a low grade. By the time they reach college it is pretty much: "Just tell me what you want."

What a totally unnecessary tragedy!

Lynn Stoddard asks, *What killed the natural Need to Know, and must it remain a permanent death? Can this thing we call education be a place where we restore learning to its natural state of being—a fascination with growing in knowing?*

Stop a second. No, really. Just stop a second (or two) and

imagine, what would a school be like if kids were all fascinated with learning? Wouldn't that be wonderful? A school like that would probably have few, if any, discipline problems. Absentee-ism numbers would shrink, not to mention there would be a no-table reduction in dropout figures. Certainly that school would not be filled with bored students and frazzled teachers trying to figure out how to entice students to learn something they do not want to learn.

Lynn Stoddard speaks to us in simple words and with natural concepts we can understand. He is the kind of genius who sees through a glass darkly and interprets what we do not readily see. He tells us gently and positively how we can have that school filled with fascinated people. True genius that he is, he not only describes the problem but races ahead to suggest a framework for a solution. Currently, we have far too many high pressur-ing, punitive, behaviorist schools that are forcing more and more memorization upon children just to drive up test scores. Worse still, now the scores are for federal and state offices of education, not for the student. All the symptoms and signs today scream for us to do something else. But what? And now enters Lynn's real genius again: He lays out the solution in such a way that we resonate with it and say, "Why didn't I think of that!?"

We now have in the United States an almost 30% failure to complete problem. If that is not a loud signaling that we are off track, then what is it? It *is* a signal—a *huge* one to which, un-fortunately, we have become accustomed. If you live in a small town and there is a murder it is all over the papers and central to local conversations. That same murder in a large metro area like Detroit or LA or New York is barely noticed and certainly is not going to make any headlines, or be central in conversation. It may not even make the evening or morning news. Why? Be-cause it happens so often it is no longer newsworthy. Just another murder, oh well, what else is new? Just because we are acclimated to something does not make it any more right or "normal."

Lynn tells us that we may have highway hypnosis with regard to noticing that the joyous part of learning has been nearly extinguished in many of our schools. In this book he relates an unusual concept that he and a group of teachers discovered when they decided to ask parents about their priorities for the education of their children.

Have we become conditioned to accept the snuffing out of the pilot light of being fascinated with learning as part of the schools' function? If so, that is a very sad thing. But wait! There is hope! We have a solution, and it is not expensive, it is not laborious, it does not need endless taskforce and committee meetings to arrive at a new and positive way of conducting this thing we call *school*.

Lynn reveals a plan to realign our schools, recapturing that natural zone found inside each of us, and it can be accomplished painlessly and easily instituted TODAY—tomorrow at the latest.

The Need to Know is naturally precious, and it should never end. It should be the driving force behind us all, persistently exploring a constantly unfolding new world as we grow into our Greatness. Let us rebuild schools to do just that. Let us restructure our schools. And if that is unrealistic then here is an idea: Let us listen to Lynn Stoddard and when we create a new curriculum, develop a new program, or build a new school, let us do it along the lines of *Educating for Human Greatness*, and in such a way that the current majority of mainstream educators will look over at us and say, "Now what is THAT?!?!?!"

—Anthony Dallmann-Jones PhD
2010

THE BIRTH OF A BEST SELLER?

The birth of any book is never a solitary journey. Although most only remember the author, in many ways a published book is a group endeavor. Because I am blessed with some of the most highly regarded supporters one can have, I want to thank and credit them deliberately. Without their support you would not have this book in your hands. It is difficult to express in words how much this group means to me and how much I appreciate their support for the EfHG concept. I wanted to thank them by including them below.

Expressly, I first wish to thank Professor Anthony Dallmann-Jones PhD, for his vital role in arranging things with our delightful publisher - Peppertree Press. I thank him also for our many dialogues and many, many hours of editing he has put in which led to the expanded and improved second edition of Educating for Human Greatness.

Anthony Dallmann-Jones is author of *SHADOW CHILDREN ~ Understanding Education's #1 Issue.* He is a professor of education for master teachers in the Differentiating Instruction for At-risk Learners (DIAL) Program at Marian University. He is also the Director of the National At-Risk Education Network. He makes his home online at: director@NAREN.info www.AtRiskEducation.Net and SOE. MarianUniversity.edu.

Laurence A. Becker is an educator, coach, author, and producer of the international award-winning documentary film WITH EYES WIDE OPEN about the life of Richard Wawro, autistic savant artist from Edinburgh, Scotland. rbecker64@ aol.com www.savantsyndrome.com

Emmanuel Bernstein has been an educator for all ages from Hawaii to Massachusetts, and wrote *The Secret Revolution: A Psychologist's Adventures in Education* which celebrates alternative methods in education.

Darla Isackson is editor of over 200 books, columnist for Meridian Magazine since 2002, including a series of in-depth articles on education, author of *Trust God No Matter What!* Web site: darlaisackson.com

Phillip Kovacs is a former teacher now teaching teachers at UA Huntsville. He is interested in helping communities develop alternatives to status quo schooling.

Arnie Langberg is a friend and fellow radical, has started schools that are patterned after the Maurice Gibbons Walkabout model. He is also a talented musician.

Deborah Meier is an educator for 40 plus years. Author of *In the Power of Their Ideas* and other books. deborah.meier@gmail.com

Jerry Mintz is founder and Director of the Alternative Education Resource Organization, www.educationrevolution.org. 800 769-4171. Editor of the Handbook of *Alternative Education* and the *Almanac of Education Choice*, author of *No Homework and Recess All Day.*

MaryBeth Merritt is the founder of The Living Learning Collaborative and Four Winds, Inc.   www.globalalliance-fortransformingeducation.info

Ron Miller is the author or editor of nine books on educational alternatives, and the editor of *Education Revolution* magazine. He has taught at Champlain and Goddard colleges and helped to start independent schools. Many of his writings can be found at **www.pathsoflearning.net**.

Beth Shumway Moore is a retired educator, successful writer of two published books and many articles. She is an active volunteer, helping to make a better world.

Susan Ohanian is a longtime teacher and author of 25 books. Her articles have appeared in publications ranging from *The Atlantic* and *Nation* to *Language Arts*, *Parenting* and *USA Today*. She runs a website of resistance to NCLB and Race to the Top. www.susanohanian.org and another to stop national standards. www.StopNationalStandards.com

Mary Orlando has been a Montessori educator and administrator for the past 41 years. morlando@villamontessori.com

Lu Pilgrim is a human development professor, project coach and collaborator, and published education writer.

Ellie Seely is founder and director of the Horizon School in Ogden, Utah.

Yvonne Siu-Runyon is a former public school teacher and professor emeriti at the University of Northern Colorado and a current member of the presidential team for the National Council for Teachers of English. She has 41 years of professional educational experiences. hanalei@indra.com

Maria K. West is a family child care provider, advocate for raising and educating all our children - birth through adulthood - in supportive, thoughtful, caring communities.

Also deserving mention and deep gratitude are:

Sheila Davis is a retired educator who taught 24 years in Washington, California, and Utah, trying to incorporate the Educating for Human Greatness philosophy of education with which she resonates. slcdolfin@yahoo.com

Michael Mendizza is an author, artist, documentary filmmaker, founder of Touch the Future, a nonprofit learning design center focusing on continuing adult development that compliments and balances continuing child development.

Don Perl is a lifetime educator; he holds a JD degree and an MA degree in teaching Spanish. He has taught all levels, from elementary school students to university students. He is president of the Coalition for Better Education, Inc. (www.thecbe.org)

Marion Brady is a retired high school teacher, college professor, district-level administrator, textbook and professional book author, newspaper columnist, and consultant to publishers, states, and foundations. www.MarionBrady.com

Barbara Neighbors Deal, Literary Associates, is an amazing book agent who spearheaded publication of the first edition of *Educating for Human Greatness*. BarbaraDeal@charter.net

Charles Jakiela, Holistic Education Press, is the man who first recognized the value of the *Educating for Human Greatness* concept and published the first edition that is now available in CD format. Csj1@great-ideas.org

TABLE OF CONTENTS

PURPOSE

The purpose of this book is to introduce a different, progressive paradigm of public and private education called, *Educating for Human Greatness*.

It serves as an "owner's manual" with principles, ideas and a framework for developing a higher level of teaching, thinking and learning in each community. It is a guide for parents and teachers to use in drawing forth the light and unique GREATNESS that lies within themselves and each amazing child.

The book provides a nutshell version of *Educating for Human Greatness* and a comparison of EfHG with conventional education. This is followed by a comprehensive overview and more detail as you move through the book.

May you have a joyful journey.

The NUTSHELL VERSION
of Educating for Human Greatness
Showing the Value of Diversity
Over Uniformity

Major Focus:
What is the purpose of public education?

Develop great human beings to be contributors to society.

"With 1 out of every 100 Americans - more than 2.3 million - now behind bars, the United States imprisons far more people - both proportionally and absolutely - than any other country in the world, including China. Representing only 5% of the world's population, America has 25% of the world's inmates." (Darling-Hammond)

The BIG IDEA:
How is "Educating for Human Greatness" different from conventional education?

EFHG is different in three major ways:

1. Teachers unite with parents to help students become contributors to home, school and community.

2. Teachers do not try to standardize students. The first priority is to nurture positive human diversity (PhD) and draw forth the unique talents, gifts, interests and abilities of each amazing child.

3. Reading, writing, math and hundreds of other disciplines are taught and learned as **tools,** rather than as goals, to help

students grow in the qualities of human greatness. This concept makes possible two things that are rarely provided in public or private education:

Teachers are empowered to perform as highly skilled professionals. They use their knowledge, sensitivity, love and creativity to meet the needs of individual students. (Not to meet the uninformed demands of politicians.)

Parents are meaningfully involved in each child's education.

Action Priorities:
How do we help students become contributors?

Parents* and teachers unite to help students (and one another) grow in seven dimensions of human greatness: (The dimensions were obtained from asking parents this question: "What would you like the school to help you accomplish for your child this year?")

Identity – Develop unique talents, gifts, interests, and abilities. "Give my child a sense of self-worth, a person with confidence to be a special contributor to society."

Inquiry – Cultivate curiosity and the ability to ask important questions.

Interaction – Promote courtesy, caring, communication and cooperation.

Initiative – Foster self-directed learning, autonomy, self-confidence and will power.

Imagination – Nurture creativity in all of its many forms.

Intuition – Develop emotional intelligence, the sixth sense. Gain the ability to recognize truth with the heart as well as intellectually.

Integrity – Develop honesty, character, morality, humility and responsibility for self.

The Role of Teachers:
What do teachers do?

Each of the seven dimensions calls for teachers to design and engage students in activities that will help each child grow in that dimension. The first dimension, Identity, calls for teachers to get to know the special needs of each child and develop a relationship that draws forth the best in each one. Teachers serve as guides and advisors and provide experiences that will help students grow as individuals, each with unique needs, talents, gifts, interests and abilities to be discovered and developed. Rather than aiming to standardize students, teachers unite with parents and caregivers to nurture positive human diversity.

The Role of Parents:
What do parents do?

Given the reality of many other demands on parents' time, they still understand and keep in mind the seven dimensions; they keep teachers informed of a child's changing needs and actively nurture growth in each dimension whenever and however they can. One major role that parents play is to help a child see one's value and to have a desire to develop his/her gifts to be a special contributor to society. Parents often serve as partners for Great Brain or other individual research projects to help students grow in the powers of inquiry and interaction. They also volunteer their time, helping at school.

Curriculum:
Is there a body of knowledge and skills that every child should have?

Reading, writing, mathematics and a great variety of subject matter content is used to help students grow as *individuals* with unique potential, not as standardized products. Curriculum is not the goal—an end in itself like it is in conventional education, but as a *tool* to help students grow in Identity, Inquiry, Interaction, Initiative, Imagination, Intuition and Integrity —the qualities most often found in contributors—and to help each child find purpose and meaning in life. *When reading, writing and mathematics are learned as tools of inquiry and interaction, they are learned with more depth and meaning than when they are learned as ends in and of themselves.*

Each student has at least one caring advisor/mentor to help guide choices. Students are guided to choose courses and content that will assist each child to develop unique talents, interests and abilities. Students prepare presentations to share knowledge, growth and talent development during each school year for personal and group accomplishments and in preparation for the final rite of passage from childhood to adulthood. Parents and teachers also share their talents and interests.

Assessment:
How should we measure learning?

Students are assessed on what they are trying to accomplish—student growth in becoming contributors to society. Students are helped to assess their own growth in the seven dimensions of greatness. Each student keeps an individualized record of growth in personal portfolios, electronically, or in some other way, for periodic review with parents and teachers. Students learn how to assess the quality of their own work.

Graduation:
Is this student ready to be a contributing member of society?

The rite of passage to adulthood consists of an engaging personalized ceremony in which the student shows how s/he has grown in each of the dimensions of greatness and how s/he intends to become a more valuable contributor.

*We are all well aware that the number of American homes with both biological parents being present is, unfortunately, becoming increasingly rare. As you read the book, remember that the word "parents" is synonymous with the word "caregivers" i.e., anyone parenting the child.

A Comparison of
Two Philosophies of Education

CONVENTIONAL EDUCATION	EDUCATING FOR HUMAN GREATNESS
Student Achievement in Curriculum (i.e., grade-point averages) is the main goal of public education. .	Human greatness is the main goal. Parents and teachers unite to help students become valuable contributors to society.
A common core curriculum, imposed by politicians, is the boss over parents, teachers and students	Curriculum is the servant of parents and teachers, chosen and adapted by them to embrace a variety of needs in all youngsters
The aim is for standardization – attempting to make children alike in knowledge and skills. National and state standards for student uniformity are imposed.	The aim is to nurture human diversity - helping students discover and develop their unique talents and gifts. High standards are adopted for developing student individuality.
Has a low estimate of human potential. Ranks people with I.Q. tests.	Sees unlimited potential in every person. Acknowledges that human intelligence is not numerically measurable.
Tries to measure student growth in curriculum.	Assesses student growth in the qualities of human greatness and contributive behavior.
Parents are not meaningfully involved in public or private education.	Parents are involved as full and equal partners with teachers to help students grow in their qualities of greatness.

CHAPTER 1

The GRAND OVERVIEW of Educating for Human Greatness

"There is nothing progressive about being pig-headed and refusing to admit a mistake."

—C.S. Lewis

In 1983 a National Commission on Excellence in Education issued a "Nation at Risk Report" and set in motion a series of government imposed reforms, all based on a false goal: student achievement in curriculum. One of these reforms, "No Child Left Behind," put extra pressure on teachers to ignore the diverse needs of students and, instead, standardize students in reading, writing and math. More recently the U.S. Department of Education has installed a set of national standards for student uniformity. Subject matter specialists, along with major influence from business and industry, have decided what all students should know and be able to do at each grade level. Tests are administered to assess student learning of the prescribed material. In some cases the tests are used as an assessment of the quality of teaching. This top-down, misguided pressure is evidence that public school teaching is not regarded as a profession in our society.

1

Over many years our culture has become so obsessed with curriculum we have lost sight of our purpose—curriculum for what? Student achievement in curriculum has become a false goal, an end in and of itself. Grade point averages have become the main indicators of achievement in education. We have a cultural cramp—a mass mind-set that spawns counterfeit reform movements such as NCLB and the National Standards concept.

For genuine reform of public education we must start with a crystal-clear purpose. In 1973, ten years before "Nation at Risk," the teachers at Hill Field Elementary School in Clearfield, Utah, decided to ask parents about their priorities for the education of their children. In interviews with thousands of parents over several years, teachers were surprised to learn of three needs that parents felt were more important to them than the need to have a child achieve in reading, writing and arithmetic. First, parents wanted us to respect children as individuals, to pay attention to each child's special needs, and help youngsters develop their unique talents and abilities. Second, they wanted children to increase in curiosity and passion for knowledge – they wanted children to "fall in love with learning." And third, parents wanted teachers to help children learn how to express themselves, communicate and get along. The priorities were so consistent with nearly every parent we surmised that these may be the core needs of people in every culture—the need to know who we are and what we can become (identity), the need for knowledge (inquiry), and the need for respect and love (interaction).

This finding led to a new concept—curriculum should not be viewed as a *goal*, but as a *tool* to help students grow in identity, inquiry and interaction. Even though the concept was temporarily smothered by the standardization movement, it remained alive for all these years and has now evolved to become a framework for authentic reform of public, private and other forms of education, and has grown to include seven priorities:

FOCUS:
Seven Priorities
The Dimensions of Human Greatness:

Identity – Help students learn who they are—as individuals with unlimited potential, develop their unique talents and gifts to realize self-worth and develop a strong desire to be contributors to family, school, and community. Nurture health and physical fitness.

Inquiry – Stimulate curiosity; awaken a sense of wonder and appreciation for nature and for humankind. Help students develop the power to ask important, penetrating questions.

Interaction – Promote courtesy, caring, communication and cooperation.

Initiative – Foster self-directed learning, will power and self-evaluation.

Imagination – Nurture creativity and creative expression.

Intuition – Develop emotional intelligence, the sixth sense. Gain the ability to recognize truth with the heart as well as intellectually.

Integrity – Develop honesty, character, morality and responsibility for self.

With these priorities, reading, writing, mathematics and other disciplines are viewed, not as *goals*, but as *tools* to help students grow in the dimensions of greatness and be valuable contributors to society.

The seven dimensions of human greatness are the beginning of a process to build public and private school teaching into a genuine profession.

ॐ

ATTITUDE

THE DESIRE TO BE A CONTRIBUTOR

During the years when teachers were interviewing parents, Davis County, Utah, was in the process of building an enormous new jail to house the many lawbreakers who were choosing to become burdens to society. This condition made us wonder if schools could somehow have a role in reducing criminal behavior. What would happen if parents and teachers were to unite to help each child, early on, to gain an identity of self-worth and a desire to be a contributor, rather than a burden to society? With this in mind we adopted a school mission to *develop great human beings to be contributors—not burdens—to society.*

We knew there were plenty of smart crooks – many who were proficient in reading, writing and arithmetic. We felt the key is *desire* – a firm resolve to be a *contributor* to society, and this is tied to the development of one's unique talents and gifts so the individual can see many ways to contribute. Every person born on Earth has a unique set of at least nine or more areas of intelligence through which to contribute, (Gardner) as well as the seven dimensions and numerous facets of creativity.

The challenge is to help every student develop an *identity* of self-worth and see a vision of using one's special talents and gifts to benefit the world. We found that very young children can learn to sense the feelings that come from being a contributor as contrasted to the feelings that arise from doing things that are not helpful. The desire to be a contributor grows as one discovers and develops personal talents and gifts, thus opening several doors through which to contribute. This is a major reason why *identity* should be a top priority for education.

❧

IDENTITY
THE FIRST DIMENSION OF GREATNESS.

Look well into thyself; there is a source of strength which will always spring up if thou wilt always look there.

—Marcus Aurelius

The most dramatic and fundamental change in education will occur when teachers stop trying to standardize students and start to do the opposite—value and nurture **p**ositive **hu**man **d**iversity. To nurture **phd** is to work in harmony with nature and free students to recognize and develop their unlimited potential.

Human beings have much greater potential than we have supposed. Marianne Williamson tells what happens when we acknowledge human greatness:

You are a child of God.
We are all meant to shine, as children do.
We were born to make manifest the glory of God that is within us. It's not just in some of us; it's in everyone.

5

And as we let our own light shine,
we unconsciously give other people permission to do the same.

—Williamson

Students start to build an identity of greatness when they begin to discover and develop their own sets of gifts and talents. One of the strategies that teachers invented to help students discover their talents and gifts was the "Shining Stars Talent Development Program." In a series of talent shows children were invited to "try on" various talents from a supplied list of 82 talents. (Appendix) The talents were performed in weekly class talent shows. From these weekly performances some children were chosen to appear in the monthly grade-level shows, and then in the quarterly whole school shows. Over a period of time, as children were able to "try on" various talents, each student began to discover what s/he was good at and develop a positive identity. The "shopping list" of talents included talents in several categories—arts, crafts, hobbies, writing, speaking, dramatics, dancing, physical, musical, and others. Also, many students tried their hand at being a master or mistress of ceremonies. Others developed leadership skills in organizing theater groups or small bands playing home-made musical instruments. One of the highlights of the talent development program was when parents appeared to demonstrate their talents.

It is common knowledge that people are born with different sets of talents and gifts. Some are good in math, some good in music, some in verbal skills, some are talented in art, some are good at fixing things, and some have natural physical ability. When teachers aim to help students find something in which they can excel, it does wonders for a student's self-esteem. One fourth grade teacher in our school had a student whose talents were hard to find. One day she excitedly reported in faculty meeting that she had found that Billy could stand on his head with his feet straight up for a long time. When Billy's gift was acknowledged he began to improve in academics too.

Another boy's schizophrenic behavior changed when his talent on a unicycle was recognized and appreciated. Later on, I tell how my son's academic achievement changed when he was given opportunities to share his amazing singing ability.

Feelings of self-worth grow when teachers stop trying to help students overcome their *deficits* and begin to emphasize the development of each child's unique *assets*. To focus on helping students develop assets is to value and nurture positive human diversity. This is the opposite of futilely trying to make students alike in knowledge and skills.

Our challenge is to help each child find something in which s/he can excel. To focus on developing differences is to recognize and embrace this truth: each person was born to be unique, like a snowflake, and contribute as no one else can. We will see how this thrust results in fantastic student achievement and contributions in thousands of directions. In his great book, *You Are Extraordinary,* Roger Williams shows how we are unique in every way, not just fingerprints. (Williams) There has never been, and will never be, another person exactly like you. When we teach to help students see, appreciate and develop their wonderful uniqueness, amazing things begin to happen. On the other hand, bad things happen when we try to standardize students.

To aim for identity in teaching is to look for the best in each child and call forth the qualities of individual greatness.

ৡ

INQUIRY

THE SECOND DIMENSION OF GREATNESS.

Inquiry activates different senses, attitudes and perceptions.
It generates a different, bolder and more potent kind of
intelligence. It will cause everything about education to change.

—Neil Postman and Charles Weingartner

Every person is born curious. This condition makes it easy to invite inquiry. Inquiry is the natural thing we were born to do. Unfortunately, the state-imposed curriculum takes a deadly toll on inquiry soon after children start school.

We can keep inquiry alive by helping children learn to value good questions. As parents and teachers we can best invite inquiry through example. We can find the "curious child" within us and show children how exciting it is to learn how to ask great questions. Because most of us went through a system that valued sponge-like behavior more than octopus-like seeking of knowledge – our curiosity took a big hit. We will need to exert some effort to get back what was lost. We can learn again to look with curious eyes and wonderment.

Every person, place, thing or event, no matter how commonplace, is loaded with new information for our brains to ponder. There are twenty-two *question starter words* that can be used to help magnify the innate curiosity of every person:

what, why, when, where, who, was, which, would,
were, how, is, do, does, did, may, are, could, should,
shall, will, can, have

Students can be challenged to use each question-starting word to investigate a known person, place, thing or event. We can help students gain the power of inquiry by inviting them to use all of the possible question-starting words in each of their investigations.

When teachers tenaciously focus on helping students grow in the dimensions of greatness their brains begin to invent strategies for accomplishing these goals. The Great Brain Project was invented to provide for the development of the Seven Priorities. These are the components and special features of "GREAT BRAIN BUSINESS:"

- Each student is invited to select a topic to study for several weeks or months until s/he reaches one of four levels of knowing—specialist, expert, mastermind or genius.

- A parent, other relative, or neighbor is invited to become a research partner to help the student become a GREAT BRAIN in the chosen topic. (See Appendix)

- The student prepares a list of questions to guide the search for information, adding to the list as the probe goes deeper and deeper.

- The student reads everything available about the topic, interviews authorities, writes letters, and makes onsite visits at locations to observe, analyze, compare and ponder.

- The student is taught library and Internet skills and given time to read, study and plan.

- The student keeps a record of findings.

- The student produces a creative product of original thinking.

- The student prepares and gives a GREAT BRAIN presentation before an audience composed of family, friends, classmates, neighbors and other invited guests. (The student prepares and sends invitations.)

- The student answers questions posed by the audience.

- Family discussions, home study and activities center on GREAT BRAIN topics. (Chapter 8)

- The student is honored in the "Great Brain Hall of Fame."
- Great Brain Fairs are held to give students more opportunities to share their accomplishments.

Here is a "how to" invitation that you can use to invite students to become "great brains."

GREAT BRAIN BUSINESS

How to Become a Great Brain
A Specialist, Expert, Mastermind or Genius:

STEPS:

1. Choose a topic: You can be smarter than anyone in your school or neighborhood on any topic you choose. All around you there are common things waiting for someone to discover something new about them. Choose one for an exciting adventure in learning.

2. **Build Questions:** Write down all the "facts" you think you already know about your subject. Make a list of all the things you would like to learn about your subject. See if you can ask a question that starts with each of these words. Can you use them all?

what, why, when, where, who, was, which, would,
were, how, is, do, does, did, may, are, could, shall,
will, can, have, if

Keep adding to your list of questions while you carry out your investigation.

3. **Study:** Gather information about your subject. Study intensely with your eyes – draw or paint pictures of your subject. Count, weigh, measure, collect and compare. Search in all possible places – libraries, newspapers, magazines,

television, interviews with authorities, etc. Read everything you can get your hands on. Write letters for information. Perform experiments. Keep a notebook of your findings. Make a bibliography of your sources of information.

4. **Imagine, Create, Invent:** After filling your mind with information about your subject, use your own ideas to create or invent an original product – a story, a poem, a work of art, a piece of music, a construction, etc.

5. **Prepare to Share:** Think of a creative, interesting way to share your Great Brain knowledge with your class, relatives and friends. Take time to prepare visual aids, a speech, a PowerPoint presentation, a demonstration or other ways to share your knowledge that will hold the attention and interest of your audience.

6. **Share:** Schedule a time and place for sharing your Great Brain knowledge. Make invitations for those who you would like to come to your presentation. Practice giving your presentation to a friend or family member in a loud, clear voice. Hear suggestions for improvement. When you feel confident, give your presentation. Welcome your listeners, and, at the end, let audience members ask questions. Don't be afraid to say, "I don't know," if you don't know the answer. Thank everyone for attending.

ॐ

INTERACTION

THE THIRD DIMENSION OF GREATNESS.

Eight major world religions espouse the need for people to respect, care for, and love one another—to treat others as we would like to be treated. Yet, sadly, this tenet seems to be much neglected.

The power to interact with others may be directly related to growth in the first two dimensions of greatness, identity and inquiry. For example, the ability to listen and respect the opinions of others depends, to a large degree, on how we feel about ourselves and others. Do we really understand the great potential in us and in them? Do we have enough self-esteem and humility to want to learn from the ideas of other people? Do we care enough to listen intently—to really want to understand why their opinions are different from ours? Do we know how to ask questions that do not offend?

Of the many ways human greatness can be manifested, interaction may be the most important. Is human intelligence manifest in how people treat one another? Is it smart to be kind and considerate of others? Is it cool to communicate? It is through interaction that contributive behavior is most often manifested. Schools have a vital role to play in helping students interact respectfully. Bullying, dropouts and gang membership are related to a deficit in self-esteem that often results from a failure of the school or home to help a child discover and develop individual talents as well as learn how to respectfully interact with others.

Great teaching starts with getting to know the student. This is a well known maxim in education. A major obstacle in traditional education is a fixed curriculum that is imposed on teachers to impose on students. Most government-managed school systems decide what all students should know and be able to do at each grade level. Nearly all state-managed school systems go against the wise words of Ralph Waldo Emerson:

> *The secret of education lies in respecting the pupil.*
> *It is not for you to choose, what he shall know,*
> *what he shall do. It is chosen and foreordained,*
> *and only he knows the key to his own secret.*

Cooperation is better than competition in learning. Students working in teams to help one another work on projects, problems and investigations, helps them build the powers of interaction as well as the powers of identity and inquiry.

Another significant strategy teachers invented for helping students engage in written interaction is The School Post Office. It's a powerful tool for helping students learn to read and write. (See near the end of Chapter 8)

❧

INITIATIVE
THE FOURTH DIMENSION OF GREATNESS

The human will, that force unseen,
The offspring of a deathless soul,
Can hew a way to any goal,
Though walls of Granite intervene.
Be not impatient in delay,
But wait as one who understands;
When spirit rises and commands,
The Gods are ready to obey.

—James Allen

The power of initiative is closely related to the power of inquiry. If a student is determined to know something and exerts his *will* to do so, there is very little that can be done to stop him from learning it. This is why inquiry-centered classes are so effective. If a group of students picks a topic from a list, they can easily delve deeply into the topic and thus develop both inquiry and initiative through the following process:

Invite students to list on a chalk or white board everything they already know about the topic. Almost immediately, disagreements will appear. This is where the fun begins and sets the stage for the second step.

13

- List all the questions students would like to learn about the topic.
- Make a list of possible places to search for answers.
- Invite students to search for answers either individually or in small groups.
- Return to report findings.
- Develop more questions.
- Repeat the process until interest fades or a new direction is discovered.

There are many ways to foster self-directed learning. The Great Brain Project has already been mentioned, but the main principle is for a teacher to be mindful of students' interests and encourage students to pursue the development of their own knowledge.

I first learned about *initiative* from a supervising teacher under whom I served as an intern. Once each week for a half day he would give his students "initiative time" to study whatever they wanted. When I tried this as a teacher it became so successful that we expanded to a full day and then more as students became engaged in investigating and developing their own projects.

The human will is a powerful force that we can nurture in students if we, as teachers, will provide choices, freedom, and help students be responsible for their own learning and behavior. The motivation to learn is an innate condition of the human race. The least we can do is nothing to inhibit it.

ॐ

IMAGINATION
THE FIFTH DIMENSION OF GREATNESS

Imagination is more important than knowledge.
Knowledge is limited. Imagination circles the world.

—Albert Einstein

Imagination is the mother of creativity. It is the ability to form images and ideas in the mind, especially of things never seen or never experienced. The power of imagination and creativity may be the most highly prized ability in any field of endeavor. It is another skill that is most important for teachers to nurture.

Michael Ballam, a professor of music education at Utah State University, demonstrates how involving children in music and the arts actually stimulates imagination and creativity which, in turn, feeds the ability to learn in all other areas. He is co-creator of *Opera by Children* in which children write librettos, compose music, design sets and costumes, and perform their own original works. (Ballam)

The elements of creativity are sometimes demonstrated through fluency and flexibility in thinking. How many uses can you think of for a pencil? (Fluency) How would you change the pencil to improve each of the uses? (Flexibility)

Most teachers are aware of some of the relationships between music, art and science. The ability of the ear to sense pitch and the eye to perceive color are fascinating fields of investigation that can nurture imagination and creativity. When teachers immerse students in art, science and music experiences with the development of imagination and creativity in mind, they are facilitating the development of the whole child in ways that are not possible otherwise.

Elliott Eisner, a Lee Jacks professor of education at Stanford University said, "*the arts teach the ability to engage the imagination as a source of content....they are among the most powerful ways we become human, and that is reason enough to earn them a place in our schools.*"

In his book, *Beyond Creating: A Place for Art in America's Schools,* Eisner lists ten wonderful lessons the arts teach us.

ॐ

Intuition

THE SIXTH DIMENSION OF GREATNESS

You must train your intuition –
You must trust the small voice inside you,
which tells you exactly what to say, what to decide.

—Ingrid Bergman

The heart is wiser than the intellect. —J.G. Holland.

Intuition is not only the sixth dimension of greatness, it is oft times known as a sixth sense, or the ability to feel things spiritually—with the heart as well as the mind. Every person is born with a conscience, the ability to discern good from evil, right from wrong, and truth from falsehood. This power can enlarge if we nurture it, if we learn how to trust the feelings of our hearts. That is where the small voice inside you resides—in your heart. Great thinkers down through the ages attest to this.

Now researchers are beginning to discover that the heart is much, much more than a pump. It is the residence of the human soul and the organ that identifies truth! In an interview with Paul Pearsall, the author of *The Heart's Code,* he says this: "*...we're a brain culture as distinct from a heart culture. We want to quantify everything. If we can't weigh it and measure it*

objectively, it simply doesn't exist for us. The Hawaiians have al-
ways believed that it is through the heart that we know the truth.
For them, the heart is as sentient as the brain. We find this same
belief with the Hopi Indians in New Mexico, and with the Chi-
nese; within many cultures the heart chakra, is the key to healing.
My kahuna friends here in Hawaii say to me, "What took you so
long? We've known this for centuries!" (Pearsall)

Now what is astounding and wonderful is the finding that
the human heart may be connected spiritually to the great
wisdom of the universe. It may be an organ for thinking that
is many times more powerful than the brain! If this is true,
should we not spend as much time and effort educating the
heart as we do educating the brain?

Some have called this new frontier in education *emotional*
intelligence. We are only beginning to learn how to nurture
it. Through stories and service we can give children spiritual
experiences and help them learn how to feel the truth. A question that can often be asked is "how do you feel about this?"
Do you feel that it is true or false? Teachers would do well to
give as much time and effort to educating the heart as they do
to educating the human mind.

⌘

INTEGRITY
THE SEVENTH DIMENSION OF GREATNESS

This above all: to thine own self be true,
And it must follow as the night the day,
Thou canst not be false to any man.

—Polonius in Hamlet by Shakespeare

Integrity is inextricably linked to intuition. It is in the heart
that we know truth. Children can be helped to learn how to

feel the truth and act on it even if it is painful to face up to a mistake. This is especially true if a child is developing an identity with self-worth and wanting to be a contributor to the school, home or community. It takes courage sometimes to admit a wrongdoing—but it is much easier if the child has a strong self-image (identity) from building up a bank of good deeds to weigh against the hurtful ones.

How do we teach integrity? The first part is for teachers to face themselves with honesty and do and say things that are consistent with heartfelt truth. The second part is to ask questions that will help children feel truth in their hearts and act on it.

Much has been said lately about helping children develop character. Character is the sum total of all the positive qualities of human greatness, but they are all rooted in integrity. The Character Education Network lists these character traits: responsibility, perseverance, caring, self-discipline, citizenship, honesty, courage, fairness, respect, integrity and patriotism. (Character) You will notice that all of these are included in the seven dimensions of human greatness.

If we want to keep children out of jail and help them become contributors—not burdens—to society, we must include the development of integrity as an extremely important dimension of human greatness. We must help children learn the advantages of being honest and truthful and be responsible for their own thoughts and behavior.

❧

Reading, Writing and Mathematics as Tools

To illustrate a point I must tell a story of how I taught reading in elementary school. I had a typical class of 5th and 6th graders whose reading levels ranged from a beginning level to 11th grade ability. The district reading supervisors recommended teaching reading in three groups divided by ability. I tried it several times and could never feel comfortable with it. Our small school did not have a library, but we had access to the county public library through a loan program. Once a month I would go to the library and pick up three large bundles of one hundred books wrapped in waterproof canvas. The books covered a wide range of topics, fact and fiction, and a wide range of reading difficulty.

On the special day, when it was time to open the bundles of books, I would take out each one and hold it up, express enthusiasm for it, and see if any in my class would be interested in reading it. Invariably, several hands would go up. At the end of the book opening ceremony children would be invited to select a book to read for an hour. We would usually take some time for children to tell about the book they were reading. To solve the problem of never having enough time for this, children were invited to write a short book review on a 4 X 6 inch file card and put it in the card file, especially if they found a book that was exciting to them. The file was always available for children to read the reviews of their classmates to help them find a new book to read. Students soon discovered that it was important to write legibly so others could read their reviews. In addition to this, I would read a chapter from Tom Sawyer or other classic book every day after lunch.

This is how I taught reading and part of how I taught writing. During one year that I checked achievement test scores and compared them with the previous year, the students had improved, on average, three grade levels in reading ability.

I relate this story to show that students will learn to read and write better and faster when reading and writing are taught as a *means* to an end, as a way to gain and share wonderful knowledge and information. They learn to read by reading and to write by writing. Later, I will relate how a great first grade teacher, Beth Moore, taught beginning reading by inviting students to label their original pieces of art. At the same time students were learning to read they were also growing in the powers of imagination. The first words to read were their own!

I believe mathematics can also be taught more effectively as a tool of inquiry—by inviting children to observe and investigate their environment—through counting, weighing, measuring and comparing hands on materials. An alert teacher can always find ways to use math as a tool—rather than as a goal—to help students in their pursuit of posing and solving genuine problems.

❧

ACCOUNTABILITY

If we hold teachers accountable for doing things that are possible rather than holding them responsible for standardizing students, we will see a renaissance of improvement as teachers become energized to use their creativity, talents, skills and training to meet the needs of the great variety of youngsters.

The tool for assessment on the next page is in the process of development. You can use it as a pattern for developing your own ways to assess your school's strategies for developing human greatness. Other tools are presented in the Appendices at the end of this book.

A TOOL FOR ASSESSING SCHOOL EFFECTIVENESS IN HELPING STUDENTS GROW AS CONTRIBUTORS TO SOCIETY

Name of School _____

I am a Parent ❑   Student ❑   Teacher ❑   Date _____

ON A SCALE OF 0 TO 10 PLEASE INDICATE HOW YOU FEEL OR HAVE EVIDENCE THAT THIS SCHOOL IS ACCOMPLISHING EACH OF THE FOLLOWING:

Qualities for Contributive Behavior	Rank 0–10	Comments
Identity – To what degree does this school help students know who they are, see their great potential as contributors, and develop their unique talents, gifts, interests and abilities?		
Inquiry – To what degree is this school nurturing curiosity and helping students learn how to ask good questions? Do teachers set an example of a curious, inquiring attitude?		
Interaction – To what degree does this school promote courtesy, caring, communication, cooperation and literacy?		
Initiative – How much does this school foster self-directed learning, will power and self-evaluation?		
Imagination – How much does this school nurture creativity and creative expression?		
Intuition – How much does this school help students discover truth with their hearts as well as with their minds?		
Integrity – To what degree does this school develop honesty, character, morality and responsibility for self?		
Literacy and Math – Are literacy and math skills taught and learned as tools of inquiry, communication and problem-solving, rather than as ends in and of themselves?		
Parent Involvement – To what degree are parents involved as full partners with the school to help students grow as contributors to the school, home and community?		

Additional comments, questions or suggestions:

_____

_____

Signature _____ Phone # _____

CHAPTER 2

Meet the Principles

We all want progress. But progress means getting nearer to the place where you want to be. If you are on the wrong road, progress means doing an about-turn and walking back to the right road. There is nothing progressive about being pigheaded and refusing to admit a mistake. —C. S. Lewis

As a veteran educator—ten years as a classroom teacher, and 26 years as an elementary school principal—I thought I'd seen everything. I had interacted with a great variety of children, parents, and teachers. With few exceptions most of them were delightful, and a joy to experience. Most of the teachers were hard working and very dedicated. A few were extraordinary and full of extra enthusiasm and creativity. Then, into my life came a teacher who was so unusual she didn't fit any categories. Carolyn Larson was a puzzling enigma to me. She was both a pain and a pleasure—a teacher who fulfilled her calling with rare charm and grace.

Mrs. Larson taught fourth grade at G. Q. Knowlton Elementary School in Farmington, Utah. She passionately believed in providing hands-on experiences for children to stimulate their curiosity and a desire to read. One day she informed me that, since she had already used up her allotment of school busses for field trips, she had arranged for public transportation to take her class on an excursion to visit the legislature which was in session at the time. Using public transportation was strictly against school district policy because of the potential liability.

Proper protocol was to at least notify the office when a class was leaving the school grounds, but to go against school board policy one needed special permission from the principal or someone higher up. Mrs. Larson was wily as a fox. She knew I was also an advocate of hands-on learning and she had heard me say, "In a bureaucracy it's easier to get forgiveness than permission." Besides, how could I deny a trip that was so carefully planned and organized with several parents as escorts and each child equipped with a personal set of questions to pursue? It was already scheduled!

I was caught between the school board and a teacher who was fiercely determined to make a difference in the lives of children. The excursion went forward with my blessings, but also with a foreboding about possible mishaps. What else could I do? If something had gone wrong, it would have been my neck, not the teacher's.

Mrs. Larson was not the first teacher to test the limits of school board regulations and, in so doing, put my job as school administrator in a precarious position. She was, however, an ultimate example of a teacher who put the needs of children above everything else, no matter what. Whenever I visited her classroom I nearly always found children engaged in a variety of activities all at the same time. Some were reading; some constructing things with tools; some doing science experiments; some writing letters or authoring their own books; some doing illustrations for their own or someone else's book; some drawing, painting, or sculpting; and some working on a committee planning a future learning adventure. Others were in the school library doing research on a personal interest. On some of my visits I would find children teaching other children about their research findings. Other times I would find a parent sharing a hobby or a work skill. Children were kind and courteous to one another and to visitors. Above all, they seemed to be happy and totally engrossed in learning. Never did I see any evidence that children were all expected to learn the same things in lockstep.

Even though Carolyn Larson kept me busy providing for her needs with unusual supplies, overcoming school board regulations, smoothing out the jealous feelings of other teachers, and providing many other kinds of support, she became the frosting on my cake. She became one of the reasons why I shifted from active duty as an educator to a new career as an author and consultant.

In many ways it was not easy having a teacher like Mrs. Larson in my school, but it was an encounter that would help shape the content of this book. Carolyn Larson was not merely a teacher; she was a one-of-a-kind professional mentor who helped children aspire to fulfill their potential as valuable contributors to society. She was able to bend school board rules because she had such strong support from parents who were involved in her class activities.

Since my unforgettable experiences with Carolyn Larson, we have entered an era in which teachers are not allowed to practice their craft. In recent years teachers have been demoted from professionals serving the needs of children to subservient messengers whose job it is to serve the needs of politicians—to deliver the official state curriculum and raise scores on standardized achievement tests.

Teachers are no longer allowed to make important decisions about children. It is a hierarchical system wherein everyone serves the needs of those above them in the hierarchy. Students serve the needs of teachers who serve administrators who, in turn, serve the needs of state and federal government officials.

Where is Mrs. Larson? She is now working in her son's dental office as a receptionist and dental technician. She quit teaching a year or two after I did because she refuses to work as a mindless slave to the bureaucracy. Her amazing creative gifts are no longer available to children in a classroom. I was saddened to learn that Carolyn and other great teachers have left the profession because they are not allowed to serve children as they did before. They have refused to be held accountable for doing the impossible, standardizing students. For them it is a matter of integrity.

How serious is the exodus of great teachers from public schools? You may have noticed newspaper headlines declaring that our public schools are facing a serious teacher shortage. As early as indicated in a 2001 article, "The Changing Teaching Environment," Hansel, Skinner, and Rotberg related evidence that the high-stakes environment associated with the standards and accountability movement has contributed to the decisions of experienced teachers to leave the profession. Joel Spring, an historian of education, writes in his 2007 book, *American Education*, that in recent years the satisfaction teachers have gained from autonomous decision making and creativity has been threatened by expanding bureaucratic structures and attempts to control teacher behavior in the classroom. Edward J. McElroy, (former) President of the AFT, while speaking around the country in 2005 stated, "With good teachers leaving the profession over No Child Left Behind, this law is in danger of disenfranchising the very kids it was enacted to protect. In my travels around the country in recent years, I've heard teachers express frustration and discontent the likes of which I haven't heard in a long time, if ever before. I hear it from experienced teachers at the top of their game and from fresh-faced newcomers whose excitement is dimming all too quickly. The cause of their dissatisfaction is the way the federal No Child Left Behind Act (NCLB) has been implemented and some of its provisions."

What is to be done? Shall we continue to allow people far removed from classrooms to dictate teaching practices? What would schools be like if legislators were to stop imposing their needs on schools and decide to support parents and teachers in meeting the needs of individual children? In such a system who is to be held accountable for what? Is there a way to transform public education so all stakeholders will be winners?

There is a positive answer to these questions. In this book I will share a vision of schooling that may be outside the experience of most readers, but one that I hope you will see as a possible solution to the search for better education for our children. If you will open your heart and suspend judgment until the end, I feel you will join with me in a grand, exciting crusade.

I will speak the truth to the best of my ability. It is a personal truth I have painstakingly assembled over a period of more than fifty years of heavy involvement in public education, first as a student, then as a teacher, administrator, and now as a consultant. In relating my truths, some may say I have gone mad by biting the hand that fed me for so many years. It's not that I'm ungrateful. I haven't given up on public education, as so many have. It may initially appear that I'm trying to destroy a great school system, but although these words may sound critical, my intention is to build, not destroy. I just want to share what I believe is a golden opportunity to transform an institution that could do an immensely better job than it now does. The opportunity is lying there, like a fumbled football waiting for us to pick it up and score the winning touchdown against what will surely be great opposition.

I realize that I am taking a risk that public school teachers will turn against me. However, I only want teachers to discover their plight and resolve to stand up against forces that are squeezing the life out of their profession. I also want parents to realize what is happening and stand up for the welfare of their children.

Before introducing the principles, I would like to challenge you to ponder some thorny questions. If you will take time to meditate on each question before moving on to the next, you'll gain a better understanding of what I'm trying to do.

- Why do we need to change public education?

- What if you were to discover that students, teachers, and parents are all innocent victims of a false philosophy of education, and that all three of these groups promote this philosophy consciously or unconsciously?

- What if you were to learn that standardized achievement tests are not a valid measure of student learning? Furthermore, what would you do if you found out these tests foster a kind of teaching that is anti-learning?

- What if you were to discover that many of the brilliant, talented people wasting in jails may be there partly because our society failed to nurture each person's unique potentiality?

- What would you say if I told you our public schools are not really about education?

- What if you were to learn that millions of people have gone through the public system having only a very small percentage of their gifts, talents, and abilities developed?

- What would you do if you found that public schools crush basic human rights?

- Did you know that student inquiry is usually not encouraged in public schools—that imposed learning is the norm that results in shallow, temporary knowledge?

- Do you know why public school teaching is not considered a profession?

27

- Do you know why parents are prevented from becoming meaningfully involved in their children's school education?

I will show evidence that the implications of these questions are all true. The six pivotal principles that I shall describe are the result of my experiences in working with parents and teachers of two elementary schools that ultimately decided to employ an unusual idea. We found a way to view student achievement in curriculum, not as a *goal*, but as a *means* of accomplishing a higher, ultimate purpose: human greatness. This perspective allowed us to focus on the needs of individual learners rather than on the needs of politicians and business leaders.

Perhaps the most important outcome of a focus on nurturing human greatness was the change that began to unfold as teachers and parents discovered new roles. They came to realize that great human beings are a responsibility of both the home and the school, and that by working together much more can be accomplished than when each of these institutions works separately. By focusing on human greatness we make possible an unprecedented alliance between parents and teachers, an alliance that results in parents becoming full partners with teachers. This new purpose for education makes a remarkable difference.

It is my desire that this book be a guidebook for individuals and small groups to begin a process of overcoming the well-meaning tyranny of legislatures trying to do a good thing with bad information. As you consider each principle you may be shocked and dismayed to discover the possibility that our present system of public education is pointed in the wrong direction. During the last few years our schools have been taken over by a political/corporate philosophy that damages our children and youth. I believe you will anguish, as I have, over the great mystery of how smart parents and teachers could allow themselves to get caught up in a movement that is so patently wrong. As you examine and ponder each of the six principles, decide for yourself if it is true. Then ask yourself, is this as serious as it appears? If so, what am I going to do about it? Shall I sit on the sidelines and let the federal government and state legislatures continue to ravage the schools, or shall I become a powerful agent on behalf of children to change the course?

⁊⊱

The Six Pivotal Principles

Every four years our political system requires a national election. Each party works very hard to develop "planks in their platform" at the national political conventions, each "plank" representing a critical principle the party believes in deeply. The "planks" are seen as the foundation that will guide the decision-making and utilization of resources for the coming administration. These principles are deliberately established priorities of great importance. In education we also need principles to guide us toward growth and progress.

Our principle planks in education in the past seem to escape us. Depending on who you talk to, they may vary quite a bit. *We need to be clear about our guidance system of principles if we are to make progress.* Following are Six Pivotal Principles, upon which to build our platform. As you consider each principle proposed here, you may begin to feel uncomfortable. You may feel these principles are so obvious you will wonder why we haven't been following them all along. If you are a teacher, you may feel you are already following them. Or you may feel angry and frustrated because the bureaucratic, hierarchical system doesn't allow you to do what you know is best for children. Please understand that the brief introduction here is only a summary of each principle. The remaining chapters will provide what is needed for you to assimilate the principles and become a powerful change agent—both for yourself and for your community.

❧

Value Positive Human Diversity

This is the foundation principle upon which the others are built. For many years the mission of public education has been that of standardizing students, of diligently trying to make children alike in knowledge and skills. I will show the value of taking the opposite approach — of nurturing each child as a special person to develop their unique gifts, talents, abilities, and skills that can be developed to benefit society.

❧

Draw Forth Potential

This principle recognizes that each child is unique with a unique set of gifts and talents. These special assets can only be accessed through a process of loving interaction. It is a process of bringing out the best that is in each person. *Drawing forth* is the opposite of trying to fill students with information. It requires an entirely different set of skills. In contrast to traditional education, which focuses on helping children overcome *deficits*, this principle works on helping children build on their unique *assets*.

❧

Respect Autonomy

In our traditional system students are not encouraged to be responsible for their own education. This principle recognizes that, regardless of what others do or say, each person ultimately decides for himself what information or influences s/he will use for growth. I will invite readers to respect the inalienable right of every person to be responsible for his or her own learning and behavior. When learners are freed from coercion and given responsibility for their own learning, amazing things happen.

❧

Invite Inquiry

In Chapter Eight I show the difference between imposed, compulsory learning and education that is the result of personal inquiry. The first is shallow and temporary. The second is deep and enduring. When a synthetic, packaged curriculum is imposed on teachers to impose on students it often squelches personal inquiry. On the other hand, pursuing personal interests invites students to ask questions and seek knowledge and wisdom.

❧

Support Professionalism

Teachers in public education are told what to teach and, often, even how to teach. In Chapter Nine we examine what happens when teachers are no longer treated as workers on an educational assembly line, but as creative professionals who know how to diagnose the needs of each child, work with parents, and nurture positive diversity. With this view, teaching becomes a true profession and a delicate art, a sensitive, creative endeavor that responds to the special, striving needs of each child.

❧

CommUNITY for Great Schools

In Chapter Ten we look at what happens when parents and teachers become full partners to help children grow in greatness. The traditional role of parents as spectators on the educational sidelines can be changed to that of active team partners united with teachers to help children realize their amazing potential as valuable contributors to society.

Now, if you can at least accept the *possibility* that these principles are true, and hold them in mind, I would like to explain some of the reasons why public education got so badly off course. To change our system, it will help to know how we arrived at our present condition.

CHAPTER 3

Public Education Gone Awry

By reducing education to a numbers game,
the standardizers and the testers will ensure
that very little goes on in America's classrooms
except test preparation.
In other words, the test frenzy will create a dumber,
not a smarter America.

— Peter Cookson

Mike Hirschi has a big heart. Unfortunately, he is another casualty of an education system that has turned away from the needs of students in favor of the needs of misguided politicians. Mike almost left teaching because he could take no more administrative abuse, but let me tell you what he did before his spirit was crushed.

Mike was a high school media specialist. He was in charge of the school's library/computer center. Mike's passion was to take wayward youth under his wing and help each one find a "personal quest," and in so doing find a reason to stay in school. One young man, David, had a lifelong dream to become a fireman. Since none of the required courses seemed to fit David's idea of what he needed, he started sloughing classes. Luckily for David, Mike Hirschi became a safety net

33

who arranged with the local fire chief and the school administration for David to spend time learning from the fire fighters at the nearby fire station.

Getting credit was the hard part. The administration and possessive teachers argued over whether the study of fire safety could claim credit in any of the established disciplines. It didn't seem to fit anywhere in the curriculum. The problem was finally solved when the school leaders decided to offer an official course in fire safety. The course became one of the most popular and David went on to realize his dream as a highly qualified firefighter and fire safety specialist.

State curriculum specialists may still be arguing as to whether fire safety should be allowed for graduation from high school. David didn't care. He got what he needed without graduating.

Another of Mike Hirschi's rescues was a young lady who refused to go to any classes. She had a phobia of being with large groups of her peers. Mike met with Judy and her mother and found that Judy was interested in the history and development of the first transcontinental railroad. She was fascinated with the hundreds of Chinese laborers and the famous "golden spike" ceremony that connected east and west near the small town of Corrine, Utah. Mike arranged for Judy to officially miss classes at school and study at the Union Station Museum in Ogden, not far from her home. As part of her project Judy prepared an impressive presentation of what she learned. For this she received recognition from students and teachers, and a new outlook toward education.

I never learned how school administration solved the credit problem with Judy. Railroad history may have been an easier fit into the curriculum than firefighting, but my point is that traditional curriculum is not designed to fit the needs of students. Instead of shaping curriculum to fit the needs of students, our system tries to make students fit the curriculum. I am reminded of the story about a school faculty that spent the summer designing a beautiful curriculum only to find out, when school started in the fall, the wrong kids showed up.

I need to relate a final story of another young man who was saved by Mike Hirschi. Steven was a pitiful loner who roamed the school hallways with stooped shoulders and a sad countenance. He was ignored by everyone except Mr. Hirschi, who figuratively put an arm around Steven, taught him the beginning steps of computer programming, and arranged for Steven to be excused from classes he wasn't attending anyway in order to spend time in the media center. With encouragement from Mr. Hirschi, Steven created a computer program showing how motor vehicles could be modified to burn natural gas. I was invited to one of Steven's presentations and was not surprised to learn that a local company was negotiating with Steven to use his program to teach the advantages of using natural gas to power cars and trucks.

After Steven gave several demonstrations to various interested groups, his personality changed. He became a popular "somebody" who walked with his head up, cheerful and friendly. He was transformed through the efforts of a marvelous teacher who cared enough to bring another potential delinquent out of his shell.

By the time this book is published Mike Hirschi may no longer be working his magic with troubled youth. A new principal decided to strictly enforce the state curriculum, effectively preventing Mike from using his personal quest program with misfits. He became demoralized and almost quit his job rather than lose his health fighting a losing battle.

Fortunately, the new principal was soon replaced and Mike decided to stay one more year. Even so, it appears that state standardization may still win the battle. Mike may soon join a host of other extraordinary teachers who have left the public school system to pursue other interests. When I last talked with him, Mike told me he didn't know if he could survive another year.

What can we learn from Mike Hirschi and what he did with potential dropouts? In some areas of our country almost 50% of students never graduate from high school. Many of them engage in drugs, bullying, gangs, crime and many kinds of deviant behavior. They often become burdens to society. Dr. Hirschi's experiences highlight two big "exodus" problems that can be solved by adopting "educating for human greatness." One is the exodus of students from school before graduation and the other is the exodus of good teachers from the teaching profession.

The solution seems obvious. Provide opportunities for teachers to make curriculum fit the needs of students. Perhaps the main lesson we learn from Mr. Hirschi is that most "at risk" students can be saved with a different approach to their education. What would happen if we decided that each student is more important than a fixed, predetermined curriculum? What if we decided to make the subject matter content fit the special needs of each student as Mike did?

Why are some of our best teachers leaving public schools and why is there such a proliferation of charter and private schools and homeschooling? How did we drift off course? Gaining a clear understanding of the problem may help us change focus and make the necessary correction more effectively and with greater zeal.

᠀

TRADITION AND APATHY

Many years ago I saw a film that made a lasting impression on my soul. *Fiddler On the Roof* is the story of a Jewish family in prewar Russia. The main character is Tevye, a lovable, God-fearing man trying to do what is best for his family. The fiddler is a symbol of Jewish traditions — traditions so powerful and enduring that they have shaped the lives of Jewish people for many generations. In an opening scene, Tevye explains, with much power and conviction, why the fiddler stays on the roof — why Jews continue with old ways — *"because it's TRADITION!"* The delightful story tells of Tevye's struggle to hold on to cherished traditions while his community is thrust into the 20th Century.

Soon after seeing the movie, I made a 35 mm filmstrip about public education's struggle to hold on to obsolete traditions in the face of better research-proven ways. I called it *Children on the Roof.* The opening line was patterned after the words of Tevye: "Children on the roof. Sounds crazy, huh? But, here in the big red schoolhouse you might say that each of us is a child on the roof trying to scratch out a pleasant simple tune without losing our balance. Why do we stay up there? Because it's TRADITION!"

The message of my filmstrip -- that tradition prevents us from changing public education in fundamental ways is as true today as it was thirty years ago. Our society desperately clings to tradition. We love the status quo! It is our cherished friend! Our society has been talking about educational reform for years and some people feel there has been much progress, but I will show the changes that have occurred are merely attempts to shore up the old system of compulsory learning. They are not a grand effort to design a new system. The changes are in fact not really changes, but merely an increase in pressure on teachers to do things that may be harmful to children.

There are some strong traditions that hold a vice-like grip on public education. These can be replaced with positive, more beneficial traditions, if we understand the roots of the harmful beliefs. Many people in our country believe the following traditions and hold them sacred:

- A first priority of public education is to teach children the basic skills—reading, writing, mathematics—and help all children reach a minimum level of proficiency.

- We must teach children the things they do not know to prepare them for a successful life.

- Children learn best from highly structured course material taught in a sequential, linear way. It is important that children have access to the course texts.

- Letter-grade report cards are an important evaluation/reporting tool.

- It is the job of local school boards to see that the state curriculum is taught in the public schools.

- Teachers are held accountable for teaching the official core curriculum.

- Standardized tests are important to ensure accountability.

- The role of parents is to support the schools with tax money and help as volunteers whenever they can.

Do these traditions sound familiar? Are you comfortable with them? If so, it means you may be part of the great mass of people who want schools to be better, but only if they stay the same–within the traditions we hold so dear. We will also see that when the federal government enters the public education picture, the noose of tradition gets even tighter.

❧

Political Interference

A few years ago President Ronald Reagan appointed a task force to look into the condition of public education. This group found our schools lacking in the things they were looking for and declared America to be a "nation at risk." It was implied in the official report that our country was fast slipping economically and militarily and would not be able to compete with other countries. Among other things, we were failing to teach our young people how to read, do math, and engage in scientific pursuits.

The *Nation at Risk* report launched a major effort by business leaders and politicians to reform education. These people declared an emergency and set in motion an extremely intense movement to fix education. The report caused politicians to tighten the screws on teachers to standardize students.

The pressure reached a peak a few years ago with a new battle cry: "Higher Standards!" This motto was adopted at a governors' and business executives' summit for educational reform held at IBM headquarters in Palisades, New York, in March of 1996. Each governor was asked to bring a prominent business executive with him to the meeting. Think of it. Governors took business leaders rather than educators to a meeting to reform education! It was a slap in the face to teachers. Can you imagine how physicians would feel if electricians and plumbers were to call a summit to reform medical practice?

The unfortunate thing about the Palisades meeting was that many educators meekly accepted the outcome. They didn't blink an eye or even gulp when asked to try harder to standardize students. The reason? TRADITION!

The new motto, *higher standards,* was not a call to redesign education. It was merely a summons for teachers to do what they have been expected to do all along—mold students into a common form, but at a higher level. It was a tradition that must be obeyed. The governors and business executives, without any input from educators, opted to maintain a system of education patterned after factory, mass-production assembly lines. In this system educators are not viewed as professionals who can make decisions about the needs of children, but as line workers who must carry out the mandates of managers.

They must deliver the official state curriculum. Students are not viewed as responsible free agents who shape themselves, but as raw material to be molded into products by the workers. Thus students serve the needs of teachers who, in turn, are serving the needs of administrators and boards of education that are beholden to the governor and legislature.

Parents are not part of the game. They are merely spectators on the sidelines. It is a backwards-facing system in which the only ones looking out for the needs of children are a few maverick teachers, principals, and parents who dare to go against the bureaucracy.

"Higher standards" was a smoke screen that obscured a harmful effect. It is much like the phrase, freedom of choice, which appeals to our sense of reason and fairness. What patriotic, thoughtful American could possibly be against freedom of choice or higher standards? Should we have freedom of choice in our schools? Certainly, but along with free choice comes responsibility for the choices that are made. Should we have high standards? Of course we should, but high standards for what? Do we want high standards for forcing teachers to do the impossible task of making students alike, or shall we have high standards for nurturing people as they were meant to be — unique individuals?

A long time ago Ralph Waldo Emerson wrote some wise words that become an indictment of what has been happening as a result of so-called government reform:

> *"The secret of education lies in respecting the pupil.*
> *It is not for you to choose*
> *what he shall know, what he shall do.*
> *It is chosen and foreordained,*
> *and only he holds the key to his own secret."*

"It is not for you to choose what he shall know, what he shall do." Did you catch the significance of this? For the past several years the standards literature has been filled with the phrase, "what all children should know and be able to do." Governors and business executives were very serious about standardizing children. They arranged to have subject matter specialists identify what all children should know and be able to do in each subject area and at every grade level. They then had tests developed to measure student attainment at predetermined checkpoints. The strategists then used the tests to hold teachers accountable for delivering the lock-step curriculum—all in the name of "higher standards." I will relate just two examples that were described in Susan Ohanian's great little book, *One Size Fits Few*. In one state, the standards specify that *all* first graders will be able to "distinguish initial, medial, and final sounds in single syllable words," and *all* sixth, seventh and eighth graders (11-, 12-, and 13-year-olds) will be able to "detect the different historical points of view on historical events," including "the influence of new practices of church self-government among Protestants on the development of democratic practices and ideas of federalism."

How many adults do you think can do either of these things? Can you? More importantly, is this necessary information that every person should know and be able to do? You can see how absurd these requirements are. Can you also see what these kinds of standards do to teachers who are expected to ensure that *all* children can do them?

The middle grade requirement on Protestantism is so laughably foolish I will not comment on it, but for the phonics diehards let me challenge you to pick any one syllable word on this page and distinguish the initial, medial, and final sounds that it contains. Can you do it with the word, "*to*"? What about, "*you*," "*on*," "*the*," or "*this*?" The reason you can't do it is that words do not contain the individual sounds of the letters.

41

When we vocalize a word it is always a blend of the sounds of the individual letters. The blend of the sounds is different from the sounds of individual letters. What about the one-syllable words "laugh" or could"?

Do you see how it confuses and frustrates children to be expected to do impossible things, and why many of them learn to hate reading? These are just two examples of thousands of similar standards that have been concocted by subject matter specialists. If you have ever seen anything more cleverly designed to take the joy out of learning, I'd be surprised. Along with ridiculous, impossible standards comes the inevitable standardized achievement test batteries designed to hold teachers accountable. Accountable for what? It would appear, although I know this is not the intention, that legislatures are trying to hold teachers accountable for destroying children's natural zest for learning.

This great pressure on teachers to standardize students has had a demoralizing effect. They know it's not possible to do what they are being required to do. At the same time, teachers do not realize they have the power to overcome the absurd demands, so many meekly succumb or leave the profession to seek more satisfying employment with higher pay.

I believe one of the main reasons we have the greatest teacher shortage in our history is not primarily because of low salaries, but society's low view of the teaching profession and the lack of trust and respect that results from it. Teachers who remain in the system out of great love for children try to make the best of the adverse conditions, but they are still affected. The saddest part is that students are the ones who have suffered the most, not only from pressures to conform, but also from lost opportunities to blossom as unique individuals. Alfie Kohn, a prominent educational critic describes the problem as follows: "We are facing an educational emergency in this country. The intellectual life is being squeezed out of schools — or at least prevented from developing in schools — as tests take over the curriculum. Punitive consequences are being meted out on the basis of manifestly inadequate and inappropriate exams. Children are literally becoming sick with fear over their scores. Massive numbers of students — particularly low-income and minority students — may be pushed out of school altogether."

The publication each year of standardized achievement test scores in major newspapers is done to foster competition and hold teachers accountable. The saddest part of this is that people do not recognize the mounting tragedy. They fail to see that we are putting teachers, principals, parents, and especially children, into an untenable situation. It's a great mystery why so many people, especially smart governors and legislators, do not know that it is literally impossible to standardize children who are each a unique creation.

There are many signs that the increased pressure on teachers to standardize students is harmful. Because schools do not nurture positive differences, our youth are displaying differences in other ways, some of them not so positive. There is a growing youth rebellion against uniformity. Many schools are stagnating, and we see an exodus to private schools, home schools, and charter schools. Some students are dropping out altogether, even dropping out of life, as suicide has become the third highest cause of death among teen-agers. We may soon overtake Japan as the suicide capitol of the world where the high-pressure education system is a major contributor to horrendous social problems.

The problem of forced standardization is having other detrimental effects. In Utah, where I live, we are faced with a serious, good teacher shortage and it appears the same situation exists all over the country. Only a small, shrinking percentage of high school graduates are interested in pursuing careers in teaching. There are very few high school graduates who can see themselves working as non-thinking robots on an education assembly line where they are required to crunch children into uniform packages.

Of course there are many schools that profess to nurture diversity, and some actually do it, but all too often many of these schools only pay attention to individual learning styles and other differences in order to help children all learn the same, government-mandated curriculum at different rates and in different ways. Unfortunately, the increased pressure is making it increasingly difficult for teachers and parents to meet the needs of individual children, even in schools that have built their reputations on nurturing differences. There are relatively few public schools that actually have the uninhibited freedom to nurture student differences.

As you read through this book you will discover other reasons why the traditions mentioned at the beginning of this chapter are so detrimental. You will learn why these traditions combine with public apathy to fiercely resist significant changes. But, you will also learn of the great opportunity to overcome these problems and restore dignity and respect to a sick institution.

I have tried to show what happens when public education compels teachers to engage in the impossible goal of nurturing sameness. This is the strongest of all the traditions. It regulates and governs the thinking of parents, school boards, and especially legislators. We have been doing it for so long that nearly everyone thinks it's the way it's supposed to be.

Many parents remember their school days with fondness and want their children to have the same experiences they had. These memories cloud the vision and do not allow other possibilities to emerge. In the next chapter I will show what can happen when we change our focus about learners and about the content of learning.

CHAPTER 4

Mental Metamorphosis

Our deepest fear is not that we are inadequate.
Our deepest fear is that we are powerful beyond measure.
It is our light, not our darkness that frightens us.
We ask ourselves, "Who am I to be brilliant, gorgeous,
talented, and fabulous?"
Actually, who are you not to be? You are a child of God.
Your playing small doesn't serve the world.
There is nothing enlightened about shrinking
so that other people won't feel insecure around you.
We were born to make manifest the glory of God that is within us.
It is not just in some of us; it's in everyone.
And as we let our own light shine, we unconsciously
give other people permission to do the same.
As we are liberated from our fears,
our presence automatically liberates others.

— Marianne Williamson

When I first read these words of Marianne Williamson, often credited to Nelson Mandella, they made a big impression on me. I suddenly realized I was guilty of feeling insecure, and fearful of letting my light shine. Now these words give me courage to tell my story. It's an unusual story, but an important one that I need to tell. I want you, the reader, to understand that it sets the stage for transforming education in schools and homes. May my light energize yours.

I have always been intrigued with the process by which an ugly worm becomes a beautiful butterfly. I am also fascinated with insect metamorphosis as a metaphor for changing human habits of thinking. We have the power to change wrong thoughts into beautiful truths. Mental habits are often as difficult to change as physical ones because of tradition, but every hundred years or so a revolutionary idea pops up to forever alter our mental worldview. This is what happened to me when, as an elementary school principal, I discovered a different way of thinking about schooling and of relating with teachers, parents, and children. I am going to share the process of my own *mental metamorphosis* in the hope it will assist you in a transformation as exciting as mine.

Shortly after I started my teaching career I began to sense some discrepancies I couldn't understand. A strange, uneasy feeling persisted for years and then a mind-altering event occurred. I was serving as immediate past president on the Board of Directors of the Utah Association for Supervision and Curriculum Development.

In 1972 the "Back to Basics" movement was getting up a full head of steam, fueled by Rudolph Flesch's book, *Why Johnny Can't Read*, and the behaviorist philosophy of B. F. Skinner. Everyone was jumping on the bandwagon to teach children how to read at younger and younger ages. This was to be accomplished through phonics drills and through the use of Skinner's behavior modification techniques. Many people in Utah were falling for what they thought would be a panacea. It was to be a revival of old methods enhanced with a new gimmick.

All of this occurred while schools were at the same time in

the early stages of learning how to use what was called a language-experience approach to teaching reading, an approach that tried to connect children's learning with their experiences and their need to communicate orally and in writing. This was an approach that offered much promise, but since it departed from the traditional way of doing things, people were suspicious and were left receptive to the fancy slogan, "Back to Basics."

Because I showed great distress over the growing popularity of "Back to Basics," I was invited to write a position paper for Utah ASCD that would give a different perspective. After many hours of reflection, study, and several drafts, I presented my paper to the board of directors. It was adopted as an official position of Utah ASCD and was printed with the subversive title, "Learning to Read Should *Not* be the Primary Purpose of Elementary Education."

Need I tell you this position was not welcomed by those who embraced phonetic behaviorism? It became a thorn to them, so much so, that I was challenged to a debate. To make a long story short, the debate was held before a large, statewide audience. It was a debate that was to make an indelible impression on my memory.

As part of the debate, I presented the "Children on The Roof" filmstrip I had prepared to support our side. My partner was Elliott Landau, a prominent professor at the University of Utah. As mentioned earlier, the position paper showed how schools are impervious to change because of "T-R-A-D-I-T-I-O-N" --thus, "Back to Basics." Although I didn't know it at the time, the points I presented in defense of the ASCD position were to become the forerunners of the seven pivotal principles for improving public education.

In my position paper I started with a quote by the great English philosopher, John Locke, written more than two hundred years ago:

This much for learning to read,
which let him never be driven to.
Cheat him into it if you can, but make it not a business for him.
'Tis better it be a year later before he can read
than that he should this way get an aversion to learning.

An aversion to learning? Reading as a business? The idea that very young children should be taught reading with phonics and behavior modification techniques was a key issue for the "Back to Basics" devotees. I'm again highly distressed that in my own state, as I write these very words, commercial reading programs have been adopted that give children an "aversion to learning." They impose things on teachers to impose on children that actually squelch children's desire and ability to read fluently. Several of my own children had their desire to read undermined by the "Back-to-Basics" methods.

Equally disturbing to me is the apathy and meek acceptance by teachers and parents of harmful practices. In the ASCD position paper I presented three goals for elementary education that were, and still are, more important than children learning how to read:

- Help children develop their inquiring, creative minds.

- Help children develop individual talents, identity, and feelings of worth as members of the human family.

- Help children develop powers of expression and communication.

Now, before you jump to the conclusion that I am against reading, please go back and examine the goals again. You will see why these goals do not disparage reading, but restore the essentiality and joy of a wonderful way to acquire knowledge through personal inquiry. At the time, I was troubled over the behaviorist movement to teach reading as a mechanical process devoid of life and vitality. The phonics zealots were recommending word analysis and phonics drills instead of helping children discover their hunger for truth and reasons to read.

With the goals of the position paper, I showed how the so called "basics," especially reading, would be learned in a more natural way that would be used and embraced as an integral part of children's lives. Children would learn to read as a process of inquiry – at the right time for each child, not imposed before s/he was ready for it. Learning to read would be a joyful activity, not the result of dreary phonics drills.

Soon after publication of the ASCD paper something happened to confirm the Utah ASCD position. As part of a project in participatory management, the teachers at Hill Field Elementary School, where I was then serving as principal, decided to hold goal-setting meetings with each child's parents, one-on-one, at the beginning of the school year. The teachers asked parents to come to the meetings prepared to answer three questions:

- What would you like the school to help you accomplish for your child this year?
- What are your child's special talents, gifts, interests, abilities, and needs that we should keep in mind?
- How can we work together to accomplish our goals?

Because it was a new, unexpected experience for parents to be included in decisions affecting their children, some had difficulty answering these questions, especially the first one. Very few had thought about school purposes. The state had always done this thinking for them. Now they were being invited to think about the specific needs of an individual child, and how the school could respond.

To help parents answer the first question we developed surveys for them to indicate their priorities for the education of each child for that year. Included on the surveys were subject matter goals, such as reading, writing, mathematics, science, as well as things like self-esteem, love of learning, confidence, work, human relations, and a place for other responses. (See Appendix A for a sample survey.)

When we tallied the priorities surveys along with the informal questions, we were surprised to find that the top priorities of the parents were not subject matter accomplishment, but human goals like the ones I had included in the ASCD position paper!

Even more amazing was the correspondence of the survey results with the results obtained in five other elementary school communities where we conducted the same survey. The order was slightly different, but in each school the top three priorities of parents for the education of their children were essentially the same. The basic subjects of reading, writing, and arithmetic, placed at 6th, 7th, and 8th, with science, music, geography, art, and other content areas further down the line.

The top three priorities of parents for the education of their children were first, individual talents, gifts, confidence, and self-esteem; second, communication, respect, and getting along; and third, curiosity, passion for learning, and work. Serendipitously, I noticed that the priority groupings could be labeled with three "I" words, identity, interaction, and inquiry:

- **Identity**: Individual talents and gifts, confidence, and self-esteem.
- **Interaction**: Communication, respect, and getting along.
- **Inquiry**: Curiosity, passion for learning and work.

It was an exciting discovery for me to learn that the parents' priorities could be condensed into three words! These key words—identity, interaction, and inquiry—became catalysts for us to focus our attention away from the needs of politicians to the needs of children. When we focus on clear goals, the human brain begins to create, even while we sleep, strategies for accomplishing the goals. It is a wonderful, miraculous process!

We became enthralled with this process when we discovered a story, "Ordinary Olympians," by Marilyn King, published in the *In Context* magazine in 1988. It related how she accomplished the incredible feat of placing second in the trials for the Moscow games after suffering a serious spinal injury in an automobile accident that had left her unable to walk. Lying in a hospital bed in traction and unable to train, Marilyn spent much of the next few months viewing films of her pentathlon events and forming mental images of how she would perform when she got well. We were inspired by her words:

> *We know that in order to accomplish any lofty goal,*
> *you must have a crystal clear image of that goal*
> *and keep it uppermost in your mind.*
> *We know that by maintaining that image,*
> *the "how-to" steps necessary for the realization of the goal*
> *will begin to emerge spontaneously.*
> *If you cannot imagine the goal,*
> *the "how-to" steps will never emerge*
> *and you'll never do it....*
> *The first step to any achievement is to dare to imagine*
> *you can do it.*

I hope you catch the significance of King's amazing prescription for success. With the three I's as crystal clear goals we were able to begin a process of changing our thinking about education. We now had goals that we could maintain in our minds to guide planning and our interactions with children. We announced the results of the surveys to parents and invited them to join with the school in fostering their three top priorities, which we introduced as the "three dimensions of human greatness."

The mission of our school now became clear. We would no longer be slaves to a state-imposed curriculum that had no goals. The school district had always expected us to teach the subjects of the curriculum without us knowing why we were doing it. Now we had some goals that we could keep "uppermost" in our minds to guide our efforts.

At about this time I discovered a book by George Odiorne, *Management and the Activity Trap*, which helped me understand how public education had evolved to have such an obsession with curriculum. He said, "*Most people get caught in the Activity Trap. They become so enmeshed in activity they lose sight of why they are doing it, and the activity becomes a false goal, an end in itself.*" Now substitute the word "curriculum" for the word "activity" in Odiorne's statement and you can see what has happened to public education: Most people get caught in the curriculum trap. They get so enmeshed in curriculum they lose sight of why they are doing it, and the curriculum becomes a false goal, an end in itself.

This was an exciting, flash-of-light discovery. It helped us understand how our society has, over many years, developed an erroneous philosophy of education, and how children and teachers have become innocent victims. It is TRADITION for people to think of student achievement in curriculum as *the* goal of education. The clincher on this is the revered letter-grade report card and grade-point averages used by schools as marks of student accomplishment. These devices enshrine curriculum as the ultimate, primary goal of education.

When we discovered that Identity, Interaction, and Inquiry were the top three priorities of parents for the education of their children, we were puzzled as to why student achievement in curriculum came in a poor second. If the "basics" were so important, why didn't parents rate them higher for their children? As we pondered on this, we were compelled to consider the possibility that subject matter content, or curriculum, should be in a different category than human development goals.

We decided that student achievement in curriculum should no longer be viewed as the main *goal* of education but as a *means* to help students grow in Identity, Interaction, and Inquiry: the three dimensions of human greatness.

I believe this is the first major mental hurdle that must be surmounted before we can begin to improve public education in any significant way. Student achievement in curriculum should not be viewed as the *goal* of education, but rather as a *means* to accomplish higher human development goals. Such a view is not easy to come by, especially when powerful forces are pushing for student achievement in content as the main reason for schools to exist. State legislatures and boards of education armed with standardized achievement tests make it extremely difficult for parents and teachers to view curriculum as anything but the main goal of education. The bureaucracy imposes a curriculum on teachers that in turn is to be imposed on students, assessed with standardized achievement tests, graded with report cards, and ranked with grade point averages.

It should be clear from this that curriculum is a false goal—an end in and of itself. Yet it's the force behind nearly all decisions affecting students and teachers. Even the Association for Supervision and Curriculum Development (ASCD) reflects our society's obsession with curriculum. When I was on the national board of directors, many years ago, I suggested a better title for this organization: "The Association for Human Development." I raised a question that was ignored at that time— why should curriculum development be more important than human development as a purpose for the organization?

The practice of viewing curriculum as the primary goal of education is often very destructive. Standardized curriculum lowers the feelings of self-worth of all but the high achievers. Many students drop out of school and become burdens to society instead of the contributors they could have become. Our jails are full of people whose feelings of self-worth were destroyed by the curriculum-as-goal philosophy. This is a terrible waste that can be avoided with a different focus.

Another reason our society views curriculum as the goal and major purpose of education is that nearly everyone believes student achievement in curriculum can be measured. Those who control education need something by which to hold students and teachers accountable. In Chapter Eight I will show that standardized tests measure only shallow, temporary learning, if anything at all. The tests especially do not measure the quality of teaching!

In the schools where we switched from curriculum as goal, to curriculum as means, we developed some instruments to assess student growth in the three dimensions of human greatness. We found ways to assess student growth in individual gifts (identity), in kindness and communication (interaction), and in curiosity and creativity (inquiry). The instruments we developed were used by students, teachers, and parents alike. Since nurturing greatness was a team effort, all three marked the instruments separately and used them as a point of discussion in periodic growth assessment meetings.

This assessment of student growth in greatness became a major factor in allowing us to view curriculum as a *means* rather than goal of education. It became clear to us that the significant measurement—the one most meaningful—was to assess growth in what we were trying to attain: the main qualities of human greatness. Assessing student achievement in curriculum was only relevant as long as it enhanced growth in individual greatness. (See Appendix B for copies of the evaluation instruments for parents and students.)

Another event that helped me view curriculum as *means,* rather than goal, occurred when I compared the priorities of parents with the three main goals that I had proposed earlier in my ASCD position paper. The parental priorities and ASCD goals are practically the same, except in a different order!

The fact that the surveys of thousands of parents in six schools turned up the same results, results that matched the goals of my ASCD position paper, led me to surmise that these three priorities are something innate within every person. They seem to represent three core drives within each of us:

The drive to be a recognized "somebody" (Identity) This drive is much more than the need to merely survive or exist. It is an intense need of the human spirit to fulfill one's unique potential as a special contributor to the world. It is a need to count for something, to have a sense of self-worth. It is a drive to answer the questions, who am I? Why do I exist? and What is the purpose of my life? It is a never-ending quest for Identity.

The drive for warm human relationships (Interaction). This drive confirms another well-known characteristic of human nature— we are all born with a need to love and be loved. Everyone feels a deep need to *belong* and have a sense of community with other human beings. We have a built-in need to communicate with others. This is the second most powerful motivating force of human nature. It is the force of Interaction.

The drive for truth and knowledge (Inquiry) Human beings are born curious. They are born with a strong drive to make sense of the world and to acquire personal knowledge and wisdom.

Curiosity is the third most powerful motivating force of human nature. It is the force of personal Inquiry.

If these innate drives are universal, as it appears they are, it means we can hold children responsible for their own learning and development. Everyone is designed to reach for greatness. At birth children have a built-in drive for self-realization, companionship, and truth (or identity, interaction, and inquiry). This makes me believe we can trust the spiritual side of human nature, if not the physical. I like the way Marcus Aurelius put it in his *Meditations*:

> *Look within;*
> *Within is the fountain of all good.*
> *Such a fountain,*
> *Where springing waters can never fail,*
> *So thou dig still deeper and deeper.*

If human beings are born with freedom of thought, they are each responsible for their own thoughts. It follows then that people are responsible for their own learning and behavior. This is the second mental hurdle that must be overcome before we can apply the principles in this book. We must change our focus to believe that children are capable of deciding what learning they should pursue. This leads to a belief that children are basically good and want to learn, grow, and develop into the best person each can become.

Compulsory learning must be abandoned if we are to help children reach their full potentiality. If human beings have a natural drive for Identity, Interaction, and Inquiry, we do more harm than good when we attempt to demand learning. It is as natural for the human brain to seek truth and knowledge as it is for the lungs to breath or the heart to beat. Would we ever consider compulsory breathing or compulsory beating for these two organs in the same way we have compulsory learning for the human brain?

These then are the two giant mental hurdles that must be cleared before we can change our focus and begin to change education. We have an opportunity to see with new eyes and consider four vital concepts:

- Curriculum is a *means* of accomplishing educational goals, not a goal in and of itself. In other words, curriculum, or subject matter content, is our slave, not our master. It is wrong for someone to decide what all children should know and be able to do, and impose it on teachers to impose on children.

- Students can be trusted, with loving guidance from parents and teachers, to design their own learning. They have a built-in drive for mental, spiritual, and physical growth.

- The role of parents and teachers is that of wise mentors—as guides to help children discover who they are, help them develop their unique talents and catch a vision of what they can become as valuable contributors to society.

- Education is the result of personal inquiry. Compulsory education is an oxymoron. Children grow in knowledge and wisdom by choosing to do so.

If you can accept these premises, or at least consider the possibility they are true, you are ready to begin the process of making the extensive improvements in education that are suggested in the following chapters of this book.

CHAPTER 5

The First Principle:
Nurture Positive Human Diversity

*One day our descendants will think it incredible that we paid
so much attention to things like the amount of melanin in our
skin or the shape of our eyes or our gender instead of the
unique identities of each of us as complex human beings.*

—Franklin Thomas

When my 14-year-old grandson, Trevor, asked me if I
would visit his art class at Centerville Junior High
School as a guest artist, I was a bit apprehensive. In the first
place, it's been a while since I've produced art of any kind.
In the second, I've never before worked with 8th graders in a
formal setting. As I thought it over, I warmed to the idea and
told him to tell his teacher I would be happy to fulfill this
request.

With three or four days to prepare, I decided to use about
half of the class period showing some of my art pieces of long
ago—paintings, drawings, and carvings in various media—
and then involve the class in a creative activity for the remain-
der of the time. I was skeptical whether my artwork would
qualify me to be called a great artist, but I was also hopeful I

could establish some credibility for engaging students in the art activity.

The activity was an exercise in using one's imagination to visualize a picture in an abstract squiggle and elaborate on it with pencil, crayon, or marker. I thus prepared in advance a set of two squiggles for each student, each on the opposite side of a sheet of 8½ by 11 cardstock paper.

The big day arrived and I appeared at Trevor's classroom at the appointed time. His teacher, Mrs. Taylor, greeted me warmly and then asked Trevor to introduce his guest. I then showed my art pieces and briefly told about each one. I tried to emphasize the opportunity we have to use our talents to make others happy. I explained how I had created each piece to make life brighter for a needy person. I had borrowed them back for my lesson.

Luckily, my brief presentation seemed to establish some credibility, for Trevor and his friends were politely attentive. After showing my artwork, I told the story of a man I had known who was extremely talented in making an amazing picture out of any squiggle.

I then passed out the squiggles and invited Trevor and his friends to choose one of the two squiggles and make a picture out of it. They were instructed to rotate the squiggles until they could see a possible picture and then use pencil, crayon, or marker to finish the picture. They were then to label the picture with a title and be prepared to show their creation and tell about it.

Now, what do you suppose happened? As each student stood and showed his or her creation and received applause, I could sense feelings of pride. Did every child see and create the same picture from the chosen squiggle? In Trevor's class there were 15 students. If there had been a hundred, a thousand, or even a million, would there have been any two squiggle pictures exactly alike?

So that you understand the squiggle exercise better I have reproduced some of them on the following page.

Now let's suppose we were to give some instructions about what to see in the squiggle and even tell you how the picture is to be drawn. Would any two squiggles be alike now? Would any be alike if we were to hold the child's hand and draw the picture for him or her? What happens when we try to force or even invite conformity? In sharp contrast to the children who are smothered with well-intentioned demands to conform, we can envision a remarkable picture of a generation of children and youth valued for what they know, can do, and become. It is a bright picture of amazing potential and remarkable accomplishment.

It's easy to see why nurturing positive human diversity is the opposite of valuing and nurturing sameness. What's not so easy is to actually live by this principle. After going down the wrong road for so many years, it becomes a habit that is hard to break. We must truly believe that it's better to nurture diversity than to engage in the impossible task of nurturing sameness.

What does it mean to value positive diversity? It means you deeply care about yourself and all other people in the world. It means you appreciate your unique gifts and the gifts of everyone around you. It means that you often collaborate with others and combine your gifts with theirs to create new, previously unknown ideas, circumstances, or products.

When you nurture positive diversity you foster positive qualities—the traits that benefit humanity; not negative, often burdensome, behaviors. It means you find some good in others, no matter how wretched or evil they may appear. It means you see beauty in the people of every race, religion, or political persuasion. To value diversity is to value people, to love and cherish every person in the human family as they

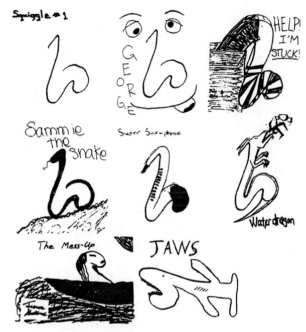

are—not as you wish they would become.

I've been acculturated to view those different from me with suspicion. This puts me in the company of many others in our country. We live in a society of people trained to devalue those who are different from us. Most of this training is not planned and deliberate; it is complex and very subtle as we grow up watching how people treat one another, and especially as we become accustomed to how we were educated in the public school system. It's a very powerful tradition. Most of us were educated to put aside our gifts and talents in favor of succumbing to an imposed curriculum. In the competition for grades we learned that conformity was much more valuable and important than creativity or diversity of ideas. We learned that it doesn't pay to be different.

On the educational assembly line we were not allowed to express our individual need to grow according to our internal blueprint. All of us were required to study algebra, for example, in order to graduate from high school, even though very few of us would ever use it in our lifetime.

We were force-fed this subject at the expense of gifts and talents that were crying out to be recognized and developed. While algebra may have been appropriate for the few of us with mathematical talent, it was a waste of time for the vast majority who could have been busy developing their own, unique gifts.

I don't mean to pick on algebra. It would be the same for any other subject of the curriculum that all children are *required* to study while a person's unique gifts are crying out for development and expression. This is only one of the many subtle ways public education taught us that diversity is not welcome. The requirements to graduate from high school are basically the same for all.

It would be an entirely different story if we were to nurture individual diversity and hold every child responsible for his or her own learning and development. Why not, as a requirement for graduation, expect each student to prepare a comprehensive presentation to show his or her qualifications and plans for making a contribution to the world? The candidate for graduation would show courses taken, skills attained, services rendered, and, most of all, a plan to use one's gifts, knowledge, and talents to be a contributor. In this way graduation ceremonies would be personalized and different for each young adult. Graduation celebrations would occur at different ages, times, and places, and distributed throughout the year.

This concept was first introduced by Maurice Gibbons in an article in *Kappan* over twenty years ago. In it he described what public high schools would be like if they were patterned after Walkabout, a rite of passage from childhood to adulthood for young Australian aborigines. In this rite the young native must go for an extended journey into the harsh Australian Outback, alone and without provisions, to prove he can survive and return to be a valuable contributor to the tribe. Gibbons gave three examples of what high schools would be like if students were to have freedom of choice about what to learn and were to be held responsible for their choices. I remember being thrilled at the vision of a different kind of high school that Gibbons portrayed. He called his vision *Challenge Education,* a vision that invited student growth in five challenge areas:

- Adventure: a challenge to the student's daring, endurance, and skill in an unfamiliar environment.
- Creativity: a challenge to explore, cultivate, and express his or her own imagination in some aesthetically pleasing form.
- Service: a challenge to identify a human need for assistance and provide it; to express caring without expectation of reward.

- Practical Skill: a challenge to explore a utilitarian activity, to learn the knowledge and skills necessary to work in that field, and to produce something of use.
- Logical Inquiry: a challenge to explore curiosity, to formulate a question or problem of personal importance, and to pursue an answer or solution systematically and, wherever appropriate, by investigation.

Do you see how these challenges restore responsibility for learning back upon the student where it belongs? Soon after reading Gibbon's Walkabout article I met a man who took the message to heart and actually organized a high school that was patterned after Gibbon's vision. Arnie Langberg became my roommate at a conference on reforming education. We lay awake most of several nights talking about what he was doing to create a different experience for high school students. Students enrolling in Arnie's High School Redirection were told, up front, that to graduate, they must show they are ready to be contributing members of society.

What happened was amazing. Many of the students had failed or dropped out from the traditional system. Since they had not had prior experience with school freedom and responsibility, there was an initial period of searching to find self-direction and purpose. Eventually, nearly every student found a quest and graduated in their own ceremony where they demonstrated the gifts, talents, and knowledge that they would use to benefit the community. (Posner) One of the graduates was described by *Denver Post* writer, Mark Stevens:

> Michelle Ramey isn't the type to get lost in a crowd, even among last year's crop of graduates from Denver public schools. She stood out as the first student to graduate from Denver Public Schools High School Redirection.

The school is unusual (no grades, no test scores) and so is its graduation: No pomp, no circumstance; No cap and gown formality. The ceremony involved Michelle and eight of her teachers and friends. The setting was the living room of her advisor's northeast Denver home.

"Michelle gave her own valedictorian speech. In it she reviewed a long list of accomplishments in three challenge areas in which the school requires study—global awareness, career exploration and creative expression. She told about studying calculus under her principal, Arnie Langberg; about planting fruit trees on the Navajo reservation in Arizona; about working with geriatric patients in a hospital; about her in-depth study of Senegal; and her apprenticeship with wig master Sami Rene Gabriel at the Denver Center for the Performing Arts. And, at the ripe age of 16, Michelle told about her plans to attend community college and earn a cosmetology license to avoid the trap of "flipping hamburgers." At the end of the ceremony Michelle's friends and teachers took turns showering her with praise."

Contrast this rite of passage with the mass production graduation ceremonies that occur in our high schools each spring, where hundreds of students line up to receive their diplomas. My experience tells me that only a small percentage of high school graduates know what they want to do with their "education." Education for mass mediocrity takes a heavy toll.

I recently attended the high school graduation ceremony for a grandson and waited patiently for over 400 graduates to file through the long line for a diploma. I wondered how many of these students were equipped to be contributing members of society, since I know that a large percentage would not pursue higher education. You could tell that many of these youth were fed up with school; they wanted no more of it.

In contrast, if we were to honor and develop positive human diversity, our public high schools would be much different than they are today. Students would be encouraged and helped to develop their own personal gifts, talents, and interests, and in this way build a vision of a promising future using their own assets to make a better world. I believe the massacre at Columbine High School and other high school murders might have been avoided if the killers had been helped by parents and the public school system to recognize and develop their personal gifts and see their bright future as valuable contributors to their community.

If it is so important for legislators and business executives to hold teachers accountable, why not hold them accountable for a mission that they can achieve? Instead of giving teachers the impossible assignment of producing student uniformity, why not hold teachers accountable for nurturing positive human diversity? The reason why this is possible is that each person is unique and was meant to be that way. By holding educators accountable for nurturing positive diversity, we return to teachers the right and privilege to exercise professional judgment about the curriculum content and teaching methods that are best for each child.

৯২

DEVELOPING IDENTITY

The greatest need of every person born on this planet is to find out who s/he is. It is a need that never dies, and it grows more intense with each passing year. As parents and teachers we can help children discover who they are and their great personal worth, if we embrace identity as a crystal clear, first priority purpose for education. Remember Marilyn King's prescription for success? When people maintain, at the front of their minds, a crystal-clear focus on an important goal, their brains begin to develop strategies for accomplishing the goal, even while they sleep. I call it mental magic.

The catch to this is that it must be a whole-hearted *focus,* not merely a weak acceptance of a different goal for education. We must truly believe that positive human diversity is worth striving for. We must understand the great advantages of constantly working hard to develop positive human diversity as a viable alternative to standardization. We must know deep in our hearts that every person is an individual who is designed and meant to be unique, and that we do damage when we try to mold children to fit a common shoe.

A few years ago I read a wonderful book that opened my eyes to a world of unique people, and how thrilling it is to live among them. The book, *You Are Extraordinary* by Roger J. Williams, is a scholarly, scientific portrayal of humans who are distinctive in every way. In the book, Williams asserts that,

> "There is now abundant evidence—I have assembled a conclusive assortment in this book—that on our arrival as newborn babies each of us brings along a host of highly distinctive inborn characteristics. We, as individuals, cannot be averaged with other people. Inborn individuality is a highly significant factor in all our lives—as inescapable as the fact that we are human. The basic answer to the question 'Why are you an individual?' is that your body in every detail, including your entire nervous system and your brain (thinking apparatus), is highly distinctive. You are not built like anyone else."

This means that it's not just our fingerprints that reveal us, but our every feature. Williams convincingly showed how every one of our body parts are unlike those of any other person's. Sure, we all have arms, legs, eyes, ears, nose, and toes, but they are our very own distinctively designed parts that combine to make a unique person. You are probably aware of the science of being able to identify people by their voice patterns and the relatively new technology of digital facial imaging. Every person has a distinctive voice and face!

This isn't all. The whole nervous system of every person is unlike that of any other. This is the finding that has the greatest implication for education, and especially for this book. Dr. Williams, the recipient of many awards for his research, found that "every individual is highly distinctive with respect to the numbers and distribution of nerve endings of all kinds—in eyes, ears, noses, and mouths, as well as in all areas of the skin." Williams goes on to say:

> "This has tremendous meaning because our nerve endings are our only source of information from the outside world. If the nerve endings are different in number and are distributed differently, this means that the information we get from the outside world is somewhat distinctive for each of us."

Just think of the implications of this for education! After the nerve endings, which are the receptors of information, comes a distinctive transmission system which carries the information to a distinctive brain which then decides what to do with the information; where and how to store it and how it connects with other information that is already there.

Every unique human brain is at the top of a unique nervous system. We all think differently. Even though we all have a brain, it is a brain that works in its own unique way. Each of us is one of a kind!

禿

UNITY

This brings us to the idea of unity as the beneficial outcome of valuing and nurturing diversity. *You can't have unity in any endeavor unless the participants value human diversity.* Why? Because that's the way we are. Human beings *are* diverse. How can we be united in anything unless we value one another? If you have a penny and I have a penny and we exchange pennies, you still have one cent and I still have one cent. But if you have an idea and I have an idea and we exchange ideas, you now have two ideas and I have two ideas. Then when we blend the two ideas together they give birth to other ideas we can share—on and on.

To value diversity is to value people and ideas that are different from mine. When two or more people value one another, they can learn from each other and blend their unique gifts, ideas, and knowledge, and make the total greater than the sum of their parts. To value diversity is to value collaboration over competition and democratic interaction over autocratic control. To value people is to value variety.

Well, what else can we expect and hope for? When most adults were forged in society's furnace of suspicion, when they learned that differences are unhealthy, should we be surprised when adults have trouble getting along? Could it be any different? What would the future be like if children were to learn, early on, that positive differences are extremely valuable? What would the world be like if public schools were to abandon their obsession with standardization and adopt a mission to help students discover and develop their true, original selves?

Once again I turn to Dr. Williams for his profound insight:

> "Children ought to begin at an early age to understand the individuality that they and all others possess.Children of kindergarten age have different ears for pitch, rhythm, and melody; each has his own color vision, and in any classroom there will be many different reactions to colors and color combinations; their taste buds will not agree; their judgments regarding a host of odors and flavors will not agree; their reaction times and motor skills — including the way they can use their hands—will be distinctive. Some knowledge about all this… would be a wholesome and early inoculation against the disease that makes people hate anyone who is 'different'."

If everyone in a school community—parents, teachers and children—were to focus on helping one another develop their unique identities, they would learn more and more about their valuable selves and the value of others with each passing year. They would learn of the many kinds of jobs and opportunities that are available to benefit society and that require the gifts, skills, and knowledge that only they possess. In this way there would be many fewer misfits, fewer people who hate their work and are miserable doing things they were not prepared to do.

When Socrates said "Know Thyself," it was a prescription for what a true education is all about. It has been thousands of years since he uttered these words. Now we may have the first chance to adopt them as a cornerstone of public education. When identity is a crystal clear focus, a clear goal, it calls for us to value and nurture positive human diversity as the number one principle for improving public education. In summary, there are at least ten reasons why we should change our educational focus to nurture positive human diversity:

- Human beings were designed to be individuals.
- Each person is born with a unique way of assimilating and processing information.
- People have a central drive for self-fulfillment.
- To nurture positive diversity is to work in harmony with the central needs of individual children.
- Authoritarian, imposed curriculum works against human motivation to learn, lowers student feelings of worth, and limits potential.
- It's impossible to standardize human beings. Teachers who are directed to do it often feel like failures.
- People have much greater potential than we have supposed.
- To nurture each child's unique gifts is to unlock incredible accomplishment.
- Positive Human Diversity fosters unity. It is a principle that allows parents, teachers, and children to be full partners with a common purpose.
- Teachers have more to offer as professionals than as obedient subservient workers on an educational assembly line.

Now, if you are convinced that our system of public education should change to nurture positive diversity rather than sameness, I will ask you, how strong is your desire? Perhaps you are not ready to go whole-hog for diversity. You are beginning to sense that such a change of focus would result in massive changes within the public system, and you are nervous and not ready to face the unknown. If so, you are probably not alone. Fear of the unknown has stopped many great ideas dead in their tracks. Remember TRADITION? Can you give up comfortable conventions in favor of an unusual proposal that is backed by ancient wisdom and modern science? Can you suspend judgment until you find out for yourself that these things are true?

In the next chapter we look at some ways to nurture the innate greatness that comes as standard equipment with every person born on earth.

CHAPTER 6

The Second Principle: Draw Forth Potential

*The day will come when, after harnessing space, the winds,
the tides, and gravitation, we shall harness for God
the energies of love.
And on that day, for the second time in the history of the world,
we shall have discovered fire.*

—Teilhard de Chardin

As with other principles, I'd like you to understand how drawing forth potential is the opposite of a major practice of those who control public schooling these days. In previous chapters I've shown how standardization erodes morale. Now I want to suggest a strange paradox.

Have you ever considered the possibility that the schools that produce the highest standardized achievement test scores may be the ones providing the least education, while those with the lowest scores may be educating best? The political/ corporate stance is not to nurture individual potential so much as it is to standardize students with an imposed curriculum -- to designate what all students should know and be able to do and pressure teachers to make sure it happens. This practice not only demoralizes everyone, but it induces a kind of teaching that is antithetical to learning.

What is education? Are public schools in the education business? If you ask anyone on the street these questions, they will likely give you an "are you crazy" look and try to avoid talking. If you do manage to get an answer, they will probably say, "of course, everyone knows that schools exist to provide education for students." Our society regards schools as the ultimate symbol and source of education. Nearly everyone feels that schools are built to provide educational experiences. Do they really do it? Do public schools exist to develop human potential? Is their major purpose that of encouraging purposeful, creative thought and action?

Many people have assumed so, and have harbored the notion for years. Because of this deeply ingrained mindset some people will be surprised, even shocked, to learn that schools, despite the theory, are in practice, not organized to provide educational experiences for students. Our public schools may exist for a different reason.

I realize that what I am about to say may alienate some teachers. But I'm not talking about teachers; I'm talking about the system. Nearly all teachers intend to be instruments of education. Unfortunately, the bureaucratic imposition of curriculum prevents teachers from engaging in the business of education much of the time. I will say more about this later, but here I would like you to consider the real agenda of politicians as they try to manage schools. The agenda may be unintentional, but it is more the less extremely potent.

Let's look at the word, *education*. It's a grand, mysterious, wonderful word! It elicits feelings of excitement or despondence depending on one's experiences in the public school system. *Educate* comes from the Latin, *educere*, or *educe*, which, according to my dictionary, is to "bring out or draw forth from latent or potential existence."

One strange thing about this word is that public school systems in America do not appear to be organized for the purpose of *drawing forth* anything, but for *pouring* facts *into* the heads of youngsters. If education really means "drawing out," public schools may not be in the business of education after all. They seem to be organized for a different purpose altogether.

The definition of *education* given in my dictionary suggests an opposite meaning: "the act or process of educating or being educated; systematic instruction." Similarly, the definition of *educate* is, "give intellectual, moral, and social instruction to (a pupil, esp. a child), esp. as a formal and prolonged process."

The definition of the word, *teach*, also follows this meaning: "give systematic instruction to a person about a subject or skill." From the word *educere* we can infer that the act of teaching is to *bring out or draw forth*. This is very different from the commonly accepted meaning, to *give systematic instruction*. Two apparent opposites. On one hand, teaching is a process of bringing out something from within the learner, the "latent potential." On the other hand, it is a process of giving, pouring in, or delivering information.

Upon which of these two meanings—*drawing out* or *pouring in*—is our system of public education founded? It would seem over a period of many years our society has evolved a system of public education based primarily on the business of delivering highly structured curriculum to students in a "formal and prolonged process." This process involves thirteen years of age-level grouping, K-12, and an elaborate system of testing to see if the prescribed curriculum is assimilated.

Our system is a teach-and-test system. Those who control the schools believe we should be primarily concerned with learning that is numerically measurable. I will later show in Chapter Eight how this system of imparting information results in shallow, temporary knowledge rather than deep, personal knowing. I will show that very little, if any, real learning is numerically measurable. I will also show there is a time and place for invited instruction, the kind that makes a lasting difference. However, in this chapter I want to emphasize the possibilities that are opened when we look at education as the process of drawing out what is already within every individual.

What if American public education had originally been organized for the purpose of drawing forth the latent, potential existence of learners, and had persisted for many years in trying to improve on this purpose? We can only guess at the amount of unfulfilled potential that lies dormant in the children, youth and adults of this country—largely because of a public school system organized to give systematic instruction. Our failure to *draw forth* the latent or potential existence of students appears to be a significant omission of public schools. The words of a wise poet, John Greenleaf Whittier, are a fitting description of conditions existing because schools have not been organized to draw forth the latent existence of learners: "of all sad words of tongue or pen, the saddest are these: 'It might have been!' " When we add up the undeveloped potential of millions of people who have gone through the public school system we find an enormous reservoir of latent existence still waiting to be brought out. Our nation has a huge human development deficit!

After we fix our present system for children, we may find there is great benefit in going back to draw forth the latent existence of all adults who have already gone through our public schools. There is still much latent talent in the graduates and dropouts from our public system that is waiting to be uncovered and developed. You and I each have a great reservoir of talent lying dormant, waiting to be awakened.

This then is the second pivotal principle for refocusing

public education in America: *Draw forth from learners their latent, potential existence.*

If we get serious about nurturing the gifts of every student, we will need to learn how to look for the special gifts, talents, and strengths of each child. This is quite different from delivering a prepackaged curriculum over a prolonged period of time that characterizes our current bureaucratic, factory model of education. We can use this principle to free people from their obsession with curriculum as the *goal* of education. It's a principle for helping learners discover their true, inherent greatness. It requires a different mindset and a forgetting of old ways so we can make a new path.

I gained a new understanding of the potential of this perspective when my wife and I attended the International Gathering of Savants that was held in Austin, Texas, in the fall of 2000, sponsored by Laurence Becker. In attendance at this gathering were some autistic savants who demonstrated very special gifts. One of them, Tony DeBlois, weighed one pound when he was born. He was premature and spent months in an incubator. Because of some of the treatments used to help Tony live, his eyesight failed to develop. His mother, Janice, was horrified to find that he would be both blind and autistic.

In spite of huge challenges, and against all odds, Tony struggled to live and fulfill his destiny to become one of the world's premier concert pianists. Now, a robust young man, Tony DeBlois can play over 7,000 pieces, many of them extremely difficult. He can play Chopin, Rachmoninoff, Liszt, and Bach, as well as jazz, swing, rock—you name it—in a way that amazes even the most accomplished artists. It's hard to name a piece that Tony can't immediately begin to play as though he had been practicing for weeks. Tony's brain, heart, and fingers seem to work as an integrated unit in a way that totally amazed me!

How *can* he learn such difficult music when he is blind? When I heard and watched him play and sing—Tony did Andrew Lloyd Weber's *Music of the Night* as a special request from me —I was astonished, no, flabbergasted. I can't find a stronger word for how I felt. Tony performed with such feeling—with his heart—that it brought tears to our eyes.

Tony started playing the piano—remember he is blind and can't see the keys—at the age of three! When he was fifteen his mother enrolled him in the prestigious Berklee School of Music in Boston. It was not until this time that Tony could put words together in sentences. It appears that it was the recognition and development of Tony's gift of music that enabled him to activate language.

This is an important point: It is through development of a person's own assets that deficits can be overcome. When we draw forth a person's assets, and nurture them, we automatically honor positive human diversity, we validate a person's self and give permission for him or her to exist as an individual.

Contrast this approach with that of a public school system obsessed with having children overcome their deficits. When we invest our total effort in giving prolonged instruction—when we keep a child's nose up against deficits for thirteen years—we cannot help but affect a person's feelings of worth. How does it influence the release of his or her personal potential? What happens to unrecognized and undeveloped assets? Do they shrivel up and die?

I have a son who did poorly in elementary school because the system was not organized to draw forth his latent potential. Doug got low grades, many Ds and Fs, on his report card all the way through elementary school. Counselors and psychologists in junior high school gave many tests and couldn't find the problem.

Then a miracle happened. A sensitive music teacher, Miss Jarman, discovered that Doug had a beautiful singing voice. Solo opportunities were provided and Doug blossomed. From that time on, his report card sported As and Bs in all subjects. In high school Doug was given prominent singing parts in musicals, including the lead singing role in Meredith Wilson's *Here's Love*. His grades continued to improve. Doug's deficits were overcome through recognition and development of his assets. He developed reading, writing, and math skills only after his mind was activated with a healthy dose of asset medicine.

Doug is now a successful self-taught computer programmer, whose future was saved by a teacher who knew the importance of drawing forth the latent existence of her students. My wife and I will be forever grateful for this great lady. We shudder to think of what might have been had not a great teacher nurtured my son's special gift. For several years we saw bad things happening, as "extracurricular" subjects like music and art were being subordinated so that students could be standardized with basic core curriculum—with the things business executives and legislators felt were more important. For Doug, music was not an extracurricular subject; for him it was the most important subject of the curriculum. In elementary school, teachers tried for years to correct my son's deficits in reading, writing, and math. All this accomplished was to make him feel like a failure, a failure that was validated by his report card. We're glad Miss Jarman knew how to recognize and draw forth the potential that lay within Doug. We're also pleased that the system didn't make Doug stay in elementary school until he reached a certain standard in "core" subjects.

I have another son who hates to read because of the high pressure tactics of a third grade teacher. She sent him to the office when he refused to read for her, but he ran outside and hid in the bushes until it was time for school to be out, because he didn't want anyone to learn what had happened to him.

It is the discovery and development of one's assets, one's latent potential, that opens the door to an acceptance of one's deficits and a desire to do something about them. Often a person will see the need to overcome a deficit while pursuing and building on an asset. For example, a person who is developing a gift in music may often feel an intense need to improve reading or writing skills in order to learn about a famous composer or performer. The desire and reason to become literate is reinforced, and action follows need.

As parents and teachers, how do we help children find and develop their assets? How do we draw forth their latent potential? A change of attitude is a big first step, but knowledge of basic principles of teaching will also be helpful. How is positive diversity best nurtured? What do great teachers do to overcome the strangulation of standardization? Extraordinary teachers seem to have a sixth sense (love?)—about each child's need to grow according to a private, internal blueprint. They see great potential and goodness in every child and know how to bring out the best in each one. They have a magic touch that says, "I believe in you." Nearly all teachers have these feelings of love for their students, but with a great many the power of love is squelched by the pressure to ignore the needs of children in favor of the needs of politicians.

What then is the best way to draw forth the latent potential of learners? How do we help children discover their dormant gifts and develop them? One strategy I will share is one that was invented by the teachers, parents, and children at Whitesides Elementary School when they kept *Identity* at the front of their minds as a major goal of education. The strategy we invented is called The Shining Stars Talent Development Program. Students, teachers, and parents were all invited to develop and share talents in a series of weekly talent shows.

At the start, students, parents, and teachers were provided with a shopping list of 83 different talents to "try on" as they prepared their presentations for the talent shows. Our list included several possibilities in nine different categories—arts, writing, crafts, dramatics, dancing, musical, physical, hobbies, miscellaneous, and other. (See Appendix C)

Over time, as students, parents, and teachers each experimented with several talents, many of them started to become aware of their unique and valuable gifts. Talents that were not normally nurtured in school were recognized as valid assets to be developed and shared. One fourth grade teacher, Mrs. Russell, reported one day how thrilled she was to discover that Michael could do something that no one else in her class could do: stand on his head for an extended period of time. She explained that she'd been looking for a long time to find something in which Michael could excel. She needed to help Michael find an asset he could build on. Michael had been a trial behaviorally and scholastically until classmates applauded his head-standing ability. From then on, Michael started to blossom in other ways. He soon became involved in six information quests over a short period of time, revealing a great hunger for knowledge that had heretofore been hidden.

❧

The Power of Love

The main point I want to emphasize here, in addition to strategies for drawing forth the gifts of students, is the power of love, the power of really believing in someone else. It is love that makes the most difference. It was not only Mrs. Russell's use of The Shining Stars Talent Development Program that made the difference in Michael, but her intense love for each child in her class. Her love for her students gave her courage to expand a prescribed curriculum that did not include head-standing.

To value people is to value variety. There are billions of kinds of people in the world. The highest, ultimate kind of valuing is an unconditional, with-all-your-heart, kind of love. It is this kind of valuing that empowers a teacher (parent or professional) to provide the unusual support a person needs to find, bring out, and develop a unique set of latent gifts, talents, and abilities. Each of us possesses a dormant set of powers, that, if fully developed would astound everyone. These powers lie hidden largely because we grew up in a society that did not value variety enough to have schools and families dedicated to this aim. Rather, we have chosen to give students 13 years of systematic instruction.

❧

MANY FACETS OF MIND

Many years ago I learned of a study by J. P. Guilford who found that the human mind is capable of engaging in more than 140 different functions, and that I.Q. tests may measure no more than eight of these various ways of thinking. We typically engage only eight to ten of these functions because schools and homes are not organized to nurture any but the lowest forms of thinking. There may be thousands of functions lying dormant, waiting to be activated. Creative thinking and other, higher levels of cognition and emotional reasoning are left undiscovered and undeveloped.

A few years ago Howard Gardner wrote a bestselling book in which he introduced the concept that we all have seven intelligences, rather than just one. They are musical, bodily-kinesthetic, logical-mathematical, linguistic, spatial, interpersonal, and intrapersonal. He since has added more—naturalistic, spiritual, existential and moral. He maintains that each of us is stronger in some of the intelligences than in others. We each have a matrix of these intelligences that is like no other person's. Gardner has accused the education establishment of ignoring the development of all but two of these intelligences: logical-mathematical and linguistic.

Another pioneer researcher was Professor Calvin Taylor at the University of Utah who introduced six creative talents that we all have in varying degrees of atrophy: academic, productive thinking, planning, communicating, forecasting and decision-making. It is only the academic talent that is normally nurtured in schools. Guilford, Gardner, Taylor, and other behavioral scientists over the years have revealed a complex and wonderful picture of human potential that is staggering to contemplate. With at least 140 different mental functions, eleven intelligences, and six creative talents, we each have a much greater latent existence than anyone has thus far dared to imagine.

※

VALUING VARIETY: MINING FOR TREASURE

Can you fathom what people would become, if schools and homes were dedicated to helping children mine and develop their hidden gifts, talents, and treasures of knowledge? Suppose we were each born to be gifted in a unique set of over 1000 dormant powers. What could we become, if each of us were to develop each of our many assets to the degree that Shakespeare developed his skill in writing, blind Tony DeBlois, his gift in music, Einstein, his knowledge of physics, or Mother Teresa her compassion? Kim Peek*, of Rain Man fame, remembers everything he reads—with his left eye scanning down the left page and his right eye simultaneously scanning down the right. He and Tony DeBlois are just two of dozens of savants who have developed their gifts to an incredible degree.

Professor Michael Ballam, Dean of Music at Utah State University, understands the principle, "Draw Forth Potential." He is the Founder and General Director of Utah Festival

Opera and co-creator of "Opera by Children." In a wonderful CD, "The Creativity Factor," he walks us through the process of elementary school children writing a libretto, composing music, designing sets and costumes and performing their own original works. It's a prize-winning program that has opened the world of creative expression to thousands of children, enhancing their learning, behavior, confidence, social skills and well being. Can you imagine how it *draws forth potential* for children to produce their own operas? It's an amazing strategy for developing **Imagination.** (See Imagination in Chapter 10.)

Now suppose our schools and homes were to value variety in people enough to draw forth the latent potential of those placed in their charge. It is a mission with unimaginable possibilities.

*Kim Peek passed away during the editing of this second edition on December 19, 2009. I would like to include a quote of his that is pertinent to this book:

"Learning to recognize and to respect differences in others and treating them like you want them to treat you will bring the peace and joy we all hope for. Let's care and share, Be our best! And you don't have to be disabled to be different...everybody's different."

CHAPTER 7

The Third Principle: Respect Autonomy

The human Will, that force unseen,
The offspring of a deathless Soul,
Can hew a way to any goal,
Though walls of granite intervene.
Be not impatient in delay,
But wait as one who understands;
When spirit rises and commands,
The Gods are ready to obey.

—James Allen

The third principle for changing public education, respect autonomy, is an invitation to believe in the right of children to build themselves with their own free wills. As James Allen so eloquently expresses it, human will is a force that can "hew a way to any goal." Ironically, this great power of free will is withheld from children when they are sentenced to 13 years of confinement in America's compulsory education system.

In our public schools students are denied the right to direct their own learning and build themselves. The curriculum is crafted and chosen by others, and is imposed on children who are required to serve the state by aiming for other people's goals. I believe it is not only possible, but imperative that we reorganize the system, that we reverse the hierarchy and allow teachers to meet the needs of students as they engage in self-directed learning. We can still hold teachers accountable for high quality interaction with children and their parents as advisors and guides. This would mean a major change from having high standards for building uniformity to having high standards for nurturing positive variety.

The third principle for changing public education, *respect autonomy*, is a self-evident truth. We know that humans are born with freedom of thought and are thus responsible for their own thoughts and actions. My dictionary defines autonomy as the right of self-government, personal freedom, and freedom of the will. According to Allen, free will is a very powerful force that can "hew a way to any goal." If this is true, we have a wonderful opportunity to help learners tap a force that may be second only to the power of love.

In education circles there's been much discussion recently about "student engagement in learning." The problem of student motivation has been with teachers ever since the beginning of compulsory education many years ago. Teachers and parents have long struggled with a nagging, persistent question: How can we help children shift from extrinsic motivation to intrinsic motivation? How can we motivate students to want the learning we want them to have? With the standards movement the buzzword is "engagement." Teachers are perplexed over ways to get students engaged in learning the required material. I believe that motivation to learn is inherent within every human being.

All of us were born curious. We want to find personal meaning in our lives. The problem with a standardized curriculum is that when we are asked to learn other people's knowledge, our curiosity shuts down and we are not engaged, except perhaps to learn enough to pass the test.

If we as parents and teachers can learn how to respect autonomy, it, like love, can change everything. The mighty force of free will can be ours and that of our children. To illustrate what can happen when we respect autonomy, I will tell you three stories. Each story represents a certain level of respect for the autonomy of learners. The stories are all in school settings, but parents and teachers should be able to transfer the ideas for use in many other settings.

ॐ

LEVEL 1: NOVICE

Morris Cunningham taught sixth grade at Edwards Elementary School in Salt Lake City. Every Friday, for half of the school day, Morris would have Initiative Day for the students in his class. During initiative time students were allowed to plan their own learning. They were asked to plan how they would use their time, write it on a 3 x 5 card, and tape it to a corner of their desks. This was so Morris could walk around, look at each child's plan, discuss it with him or her, and offer help or suggestions.

I learned about Initiative Day when I became an apprentice to Morris as a new teacher trainee. During the term I spent working with Morris Cunningham and 33 delightful youngsters, I was impressed with the love and rapport between the teacher and his students. Mr. Cunningham had a delightful sense of humor and a loving way with each child. It was easy to tell that these children loved their teacher. Love and Initiative Day became the most memorable, and the most valuable lessons I learned from a remarkable teacher.

The next year I landed a contract to have my own class of 35 sixth graders at Verdeland Park Elementary School in

Davis County School District. I spent two miserable/happy years trying to get my sea legs as a full-time teacher. I'm sure I would not have survived had it not been for the lessons of love and the sense of humor I learned from Morris Cunningham. For some inexplicable reason I didn't try Initiative Day until my third year—after I was transferred to a different school. I must have been afraid of losing control. Perhaps I didn't have enough faith that students could manage themselves.

When I did try Initiative Day it was after a period of time showing students how to make a plan for their learning. I wrote my daily lesson plan on the chalkboard, blocking out the day in hourly, half-hourly, or fifteen minute blocks and writing in the activities that would be done during each block: reading, math, science, art, writing, social studies, committee work, recess, etc.

As we discussed the proposed plan each morning, we made changes that were suggested by students and agreed upon by consensus. Planning for each day of school in this manner took about 30 minutes, but I felt it was well worth it. At the end of the day we would take a similar amount of time for evaluation: discussing what went well, what we needed to improve, and make tentative plans for the next day. In this way I felt students could learn how to make a learning plan of their own. After several days of doing this I decided it was time to try my own Initiative Day. When I proposed this idea, I told children they could make their own learning plan for one-half day on the next Friday. The children greeted the idea with enthusiasm. As we did in Morris Cunningham's class, I asked the children to write their plan on a 3x5 card and tape it to a corner of their desks. During initiative time I walked around, giving help to individuals or working at my desk and telling children to come for help if needed. When it looked like someone was having difficulty with self-management, I would go take a look at the child's plan and discuss it with him or her.

Our first Initiative Day was not a smashing success, but some children felt they had accomplished a lot and asked to do it again. Other children seemed lost, disorganized, and unable to make a plan of their own. In response to this need, before turning kids loose on their own, we made a list of suggested things that could be done during Initiative Day and placed it on a large chart for all to see.

From then on, with activity ideas posted, Initiative Day was much more successful. Almost all children made productive use of their time. We actually found that most children accomplished more in self-directed learning than they did in teacher-directed learning. Although we were still tied to the district curriculum, I found that children were freed to go at their own pace in each subject and not have to wait for those who listened to a different rhythm.

This made it almost impossible for us to return to a teacher-directed, lock-step program. I found that children accomplished much more with self-direction than they ever did when I was calling the shots and trying to keep children together as a group in every subject. They did so well, in fact, that Initiative Day was expanded to two or three days each week. This I consider to be the novice level of respecting autonomy. Now let me tell you about another, higher level.

❦

LEVEL 2: INTERMEDIATE

We discovered Barbara Sheil at an education conference in San Francisco. I was with a few other principals and supervisors from our school district attending meetings organized by the Association for Supervision and Curriculum Development. During the conference several of us decided to attend a presentation of a young teacher who told us an amazing story.

Barbara was a sixth grade teacher in Walnut Creek, California. The year before her presentation Miss Sheil had been assigned an unruly group of students, mostly boys, who had been wrecking havoc in other classrooms.

Barbara had developed a reputation for being an outstanding teacher who could tame spirited youth. Although she didn't think it was fair, Barbara accepted her lot and said she would see what she could do.

For several months things went as expected. No matter what she tried, many of the children in Barbara's class refused to do any schoolwork and spent much of their time disrupting the few who were trying to learn. Finally, in desperation and frustration, Barbara decided to try a bold plan. She announced the following to her class:

"We are going to try an experiment. For one day I am going to let you do anything you want to do. Inasmuch as many of you do not want to do my assignments, you might as well decide for yourselves what you want to do with your time. The only requirement is that you may not hurt one another."

After my experiences with student self-initiated learning, Barbara Sheil had my attention. I was anxious to find out what happened with her experiment. Barbara then went on with her story:

"Many started with art projects. Others read or did work in math and other subjects. There was an air of excitement all day; many were so interested in what they were doing that they did not want to stop for either recess or lunch.

At the end of the day I asked the class to evaluate the experiment. Some of the students were "confused" and distressed by not being told what to do and by not having specific assignments to complete. The majority of the class thought the day was "great," but some expressed concern about the general noisiness and the few who "goofed off" all day. Most felt that they had accomplished as much work as usual, and they enjoyed being able to work at a task until it was completed, without the pressure of a time limit. They liked doing things without being "forced" to do them and liked deciding what to do. They begged to continue the experiment, so we decided to try it for two more days. I asked each child to keep a work folder and make daily plans for what they were going to do. I found I had much more time to talk with individuals and groups. At the end of the third day I evaluated the work folder with each child. To solve the problem of grades I had the child tell me what he thought he had earned.

The greatest problem I encountered was maintaining order. In a class such as mine with many problem individuals, discipline declines when a teacher's external controls are lifted. I came to the conclusion that if we could survive this period, in time they would develop greater self-control At times, I had a difficult time watching some children sit idly by and was concerned about their progress and achievement. I constantly had to remind myself that these pupils had been "failing" under the old program and had never completed assignments under the old regime either. In general though, the class was delighted with the new plan. The students even worked on their projects outside the classroom. Many interesting projects began to develop. Noticing that some of the boys were drawing and designing automobiles, I tacked a large piece of paper on the wall for their use.

After discussing their plans, these boys began to paint a mural showing the history of automobile transportation, incorporating their concepts of cars of the future. They used the encyclopedia as well as books about cars as references. They worked together and some began models and scrapbooks. These were the boys who had produced very little, if anything, so far that year."

At this point in Barbara's story she told us that other teachers began to notice and comment on changes in the behavior of some of the "wild" boys in her class. They were becoming polite and respectful! It was also then that Barbara decided it was time to tell her principal what was going on. She had not asked for permission to free the children for self-directed learning. Now that she had passed the point of no return, Barbara wanted the approval and support of the principal in case there were repercussions from parents. To her delight, Barbara found the principal very supportive. He too had noticed changes in the behavior of the rowdy boys. Barbara went on to tell us about her feelings and personal transformation:

"Earlier I had mentioned how many "problems" there had been in this class — both disciplinary and emotional. This program had, in fact, developed out of an attempt to meet the challenge that the "problems" had presented. At times I felt whipped, defeated, and frustrated. I had felt that I was making no headway and had resented my role as a police-woman.

After our program had gotten into full swing, I found that I had changed too. Earlier in the year I could but bide my time until I would be able to send the "gang" onward and upward to seventh grade.

I now began to see these children with different eyes, and as I watched them, I began to realize there was hope. I asked to take this class on, in the same self-directed situation, to seventh grade. I felt these children would continue to progress toward self-actualization within the framework and freedom of the self-directed program.

Now that the mechanics of the program were worked out, now (after my authoritarian role was discarded) that there was greater understanding and rapport between the children and myself, there was greater opportunity for self-growth—not only creativity, initiative, imagination, but self-discipline, self-acceptance, and understanding. I would venture that this program might result in fewer dropouts and "failures" in school. It was not the panacea, but it was a step forward. Each day was a new adventure. There were moments of stress, concern and pleasure. They were all stepping-stones toward our goal of self-actualization."

Those of us who attended Barbara Sheil's presentation were so impressed that we approached her afterward and asked if she would be willing to come to our hotel room, tell us more, and answer questions. She came, and we spent a delightful evening with a remarkable teacher who developed the courage to respect autonomy. For me, this was a memorable, highlight of the conference.

ə❧

LEVEL 3: ADVANCED

I learned about Sudbury Valley School when Daniel Greenberg called to comment on one of my articles that appeared in an educational journal. If you watched the *60 Minutes* special about Sudbury School in 2001, you will know that this school is highly unusual and that its philosophy is controversial. It grants students the total right to decide what they will learn, how they will learn, and when they will learn it. What you didn't learn on *60 Minutes* was how extraordinarily successful this school is in nurturing individual potential.

Daniel Greenberg is one of the founders and, in traditional terms, could be called the principal or headmaster, although this school is not organized in the typical hierarchical pattern. Sudbury Valley School is an example of trust and faith in children and their right and ability to direct their own learning. It is an example of total respect for autonomy, although I believe there may be a still higher level that I will describe later. This school grants students complete control over their own learning. From four through nineteen years of age children are given the right to decide what they will learn, when they will learn, and how they will learn it.

Sudbury Valley is a private school that has been operating for more than 35 years with a long waiting list of students and parents who want to become part of a very unusual approach. "The main building is an old stone mansion surrounded by ten acres of lawns, trees, a millpond and set amidst hundreds of acres of state park and conservation lands, woods, and rolling hills."

In his little booklet, *Free at Last: The Sudbury Valley School,* Greenberg tells some remarkable stories of what happens when students are freed to be responsible for their own learning. One of his stories is especially poignant for illustrating the unique operating style of the school:

Sitting before me were a dozen boys and girls, aged nine to twelve. A week earlier, they had asked me to teach them arithmetic. They wanted to learn to add, subtract, multiply, divide, and all the rest.

"You don't really want to do this," I said, when they first approached me.

"We do, we are sure we do," was their answer.

"You don't really," I persisted. "Your neighborhood friends, your parents, your relatives probably want you to, but you yourselves would much rather be playing or doing something else."

"We know what we want, and we want to learn arithmetic. Teach us and we'll prove it. We'll do all the homework, and work as hard as we can."

"I had to yield then, skeptically. I knew that arithmetic took six years to teach in regular schools, and I was sure their interest would flag after a few months. But I had no choice.

They had pressed hard, and I was cornered."

"I was in for a surprise."

Greenberg goes on to dramatically show the difference between required, assigned learning and learning that is requested by determined children. It took 20 hours of class time, two 30-minute periods each week over a period of 20 weeks for these children to learn even more math than children learn in six or seven years of traditional elementary school.

They even learned long division, fractions, decimals, percentages, and square roots. More importantly, these children were able to use their math in solving everyday problems. Freely exercised student willpower provided an impetus that is usually lacking in traditional education.

Sudbury School is a shining example of what can happen when the autonomy of students is respected. There is no organized structure of children grouped by grades or ages. There is no hierarchy of power. Every person, child and adult, has an equal vote in deciding how the school is to be run. There are no organized "classes" except when students individually or in groups go to a staff member and negotiate an agreement to be taught and to learn. Staff members spend much of their time just waiting for a request to teach. Occasionally a staff member will post a notice on the bulletin board—"anyone interested in X can meet me in the seminary room on Thursdays at 10:30AM."

Sudbury Valley is an example of a climate, philosophy, and setting where the incredible power of free will is effectively harnessed for unusual student accomplishment. Graduates who choose to do so are able to enter any college of their choice without report cards, grades, transcripts, or SAT or ACT scores: they take their portfolios and are able to prove to admissions officers that they have the right stuff to succeed.

When someone on the waiting list finally gets to enroll in

Sudbury it doesn't take them long to find an area or two of interest to persistently pursue until they graduate or until another interest leads them into a new exploration. Students leave Sudbury with personal gifts, talents, and interests developed to a high degree: *they are ready to be contributing members of society.* The difference between the graduates at Sudbury and most graduates of public schools is striking. Most Sudbury students pursue knowledge for a different reason than do their counterparts in public education.

Once a quest is identified, a Sudbury student, armed with intrinsic motivation, aggressively gathers information to build personal knowledge and meaning. Students learn for the joy and sake of learning to satisfy internal needs. They do not learn to satisfy someone else's needs for them. In this way knowledge sinks deep into their bones.

There are hundreds of individuals who have left Sudbury to become successful, contributing citizens. I could go on, but I need to end this portrayal of the advanced level of respecting autonomy and suggest there may be an even higher level. The levels I've presented thus far—novice, intermediate, and advanced—are somewhat arbitrary. They are merely used to give the reader some idea of what it means to honor a person's right to be self-governing, not only in education, but in all endeavors. It is this right that enables a person to harness free will. It's the power of will that any individual can use to accomplish things that would otherwise be impossible.

When I suggest there may be another level above advanced, I do not mean to imply that Sudbury School is deficient in any way. I only mean to show that when we integrate the first two pivotal principles, *value positive diversity* and *draw forth potential* with the third, *respect autonomy*, teachers and parents may be able to take a more active role in a child's education without interfering with a child's right of self-government.

The apparent, often passive role of the staff at Sudbury may be an illusion, but I feel that even these extraordinary teachers are always looking for better ways to interact with students. Parents who feel uncomfortable allowing self-directed learning can rest assured that children can be set free in ways that do not stifle their creative urges. The right kind of guidance may allow students to have even more freedom. A higher level of respect for the autonomy of learners may be found when we integrate the first three pivotal principles.

❦

LEVEL 4: PROFESSIONAL

This level of respecting autonomy has probably not yet been achieved in this world except perhaps in a few isolated homes and schools. No, not even there. It is an ideal for which we can strive. The reason? True freedom is inextricably tied to responsibility and integrity. Actually, freedom follows and is the result of being responsible and completely virtuous and honorable. The more we develop the qualities of responsibility and integrity—reliability, honesty, dependability, decency, and wholeness—the more free we become. It's a matter of degree. Personal integrity is a process for becoming whole and filled with the light of truth. It's a process of repenting every day for the mistakes we make and trying every day to be a better person. The road to freedom is tied to this. It is bound by obedience to natural and just laws.

A friend of mine, Rick Salway, gave me an illustration of the principle of freedom connected to responsibility. A kite flies best when it is held in check by a cord in the hands of a skillful owner. Cut the cord and what happens? The kite soon falls to the ground. It is no longer free. When the kite is given exactly the right amount of freedom and restraint it can climb higher than the same kite in the hands of an inexperienced person—even when there is very little wind.

So it is with all human beings. Children need exactly the right amount of freedom with loving control to help them rise to their full potential.

There's a fine line here. We aren't talking about compulsion. If you obey a law begrudgingly, it's not the same as if you obey cheerfully of your own free will and choice. If you obey out of a sense of duty and obligation, you are less free than if you obey because you really want to. It's a matter of attitude.

The same is true with learning. If you learn begrudgingly, because you are compelled, it's not the same kind of learning as that which is voraciously sucked into the brain with the power of free will. Assigned, required learning has a different effect on us than freely chosen learning. There will be more about this in the next chapter, but first let's consider some other meanings of respecting autonomy at a professional level. What does it have to do with flying kites? Can we, as parents and teachers, learn how to give freedom with the right kind of loving control?

I believe it has to do with integrating the first three principles for changing education. First, *value diversity*. Just as there are many kinds of kites, each with a different need for control and encouragement, so there are even more kinds of kids needing specialized controls and support. Second, *draw forth potential*. How do you draw forth the potential of a kid? In much the same way as we draw forth the potential of a kite. We must first get totally acquainted with the kite we are flying. Is it a box kite, tetrahedral, stunt kite, two-stick, dragon, single or multiple line, delta or Bermuda kite? There are hundreds of different kinds of kites. Each one has its own special flying characteristics. I was fascinated to learn of the Millibar Messenger, a one-line kite, that was recently flown by designer-builder, Richard Synergy, to a world record altitude of 14,509 feet! Can you imagine? Nearly three miles!

To coax the most out of a kite you must learn the characteristics and provide exactly the right amount of control and freedom. You must learn when to increase tension on the line and when to release as the wind and kite give signals through the cord to your nerve receptors and brain. If you give too much freedom, the kite begins to descend. Too much tension pulls the kite down.

So it is with children. Each one has unique "flying" characteristics. I believe the professional level of respecting autonomy has to do with learning how to provide the right amount of control and freedom for each child as s/he gives signals to our nerve receptors, heart, and brain.

It takes insight and sensitive perception to coax the best from another person. When insight and perception are activated with love, genuine, unconditional love, the more likely we are to provide the right amount of control and encouragement for children in their efforts to fly. The professional level of respecting autonomy is an ideal worth striving for. Anyone willing to value diversity, draw forth potential, and respect autonomy is on the right track.

The next pivotal principle for changing education is another usually ignored facet of respect for the autonomy of children. We will see how inviting inquiry adds great impetus to the will of learners.

CHAPTER 8

The Fourth Principle: Invite Inquiry

*The inquiry method is not designed to do
what older environments try to do. It works you over
in entirely different ways. It activates different senses,
attitudes and perceptions. It generates a different,
bolder, and more potent kind of intelligence.
It will cause everything about education to change.*

—Neil Postman and Charles Weingartner

"Congratulations Jason! You have become a Great Brain! You now know more about the moon than anyone else in the school. You may even know more about the moon than anyone in our whole city! It gives me pleasure to present you with a badge and certificate of accomplishment and tell you that your picture will appear in the "Great Brain Hall of Fame.""

These words were greeted with applause, cheers, and flashing of cameras as I welcomed nine-year-old Jason Workman into The Great Brain Club. Jason's mother, his Grandparents, classmates, and an assortment of invited guests had come to celebrate the efforts of a young man who had enjoyed an in-depth study of Earth's moon. Jason's Great Brain presentation, a knowledge recital, was similar in effect to a musical recital. It offered a way to showcase the results of intense study and hard work over a period of several weeks.

The Great Brain Project was one of the strategies invented by teachers, parents, and principal to help children grow in the three dimensions of human greatness, Identity, Inquiry, and Interaction—in self-worth, curiosity, and communication. Marilyn King's invitation to maintain central goals constantly in mind paid off. It resulted in a program that gave impetus for children to exercise autonomy, their free wills, and responsibility in pursuit of deep learning.

In addition, the Great Brain program became a special tool for uniting parents and teachers in a common cause. As part of his presentation, Jason plastered the room with pictures of the moon, most of them drawings he had made while looking through his telescope night after night as the moon went through its various phases. In making his drawings, Jason employed one of the tools that many astronomers use to record their observations. Jason labeled all of the major craters and other features, told about the moon's gravity, its apogee and perigee, its effect on Earth's tides, and many other fascinating facts. At the end he answered questions posed by the audience, displaying a remarkable accumulation of knowledge. He also invited members of the audience to look through his telescope. Later in the school year Jason made an impressive display for the school's Great Brain Fair.

Jason's "journey to the moon" began one day when his teacher handed out application forms and invited class members to choose a topic to study in depth over a period of time and become a Great Brain on one of four ascending levels: "specialist," "expert," "mastermind," or "genius." The application form was a contract for parents to become full partners with the school to help a child grow in greatness. (See Appendix D)

On the form Jason indicated his particular interest, the moon, and agreed to

1. Make a list of questions to guide his research. (He would be encouraged to add to the list as he dug deeper and deeper into his topic.)
2. Use all available resources in the school and community for learning about the moon.
3. Study diligently and keep a record of his findings.
4. Prepare an interesting way to share his knowledge and make arrangements with the teacher to make a *Great Brain* presentation.

On the form was a place for Jason to sign, indicating his agreement with these conditions and a place for his parent's signature agreeing to become the child's research partner. The application form was to be returned to the teacher so s/he could keep track of Jason's efforts and guide him to new information as it became available.

Jason took the form home and asked his mother if she would be willing to help him become a Great Brain. She agreed, and they were off to a new adventure that became a special bonding experience between mother and son. As Jason chose his topic, made a list of questions, and started to compile resources, it soon became apparent that he would need a telescope so he could study the moon first hand. Jason's mother wisely suggested that Jason find a way to earn money so he could buy his own telescope.

After searching for a while, Jason finally landed a job selling Christmas cards door to door. In this way he earned enough money to buy the small telescope that he used to study the moon. After many hours of observing and sketching, after several visits to the library and the planetarium, and after much reading to find answers to his questions, Jason decided it was time to prepare his Great Brain presentation. A time for the presentation was scheduled with his teacher and Jason then prepared a set of invitations to be distributed to friends and relatives.

That is how Jason became a bona fide Great Brain—at the genius level of knowledge. Not bad for a fourth grader! Jason was only one of hundreds of children who accepted the challenge and invitation to study a self-chosen topic in great depth. His mother was only one example of hundreds of parents, grandparents, aunts, uncles, or neighbors who agreed to become partners with the school to help a child grow in greatness.

I could relate many stories of children, some of them as young as kindergarten age, who decided to exercise their amazing wills to learn at a different level than that which is fostered in traditional education. Paulynn White, a fifth grader, wrote the lyrics and music for a song that she sang and played as part of her Great Brain presentation on dinosaurs. Roger Jensen, a first grader, drew an impressive picture of an 18-wheel truck as part of his presentation on the many kinds of trucks that frequent the highways. He was so shy that his mother had to stand by his side as he showed models and told about a great variety of trucks. Penny Wilson and her parents almost got stuck in the mud in a swamp as they waded waist deep in water to catch pollywogs for Penny's study of frogs. These are just a small sample of the hundreds who engaged in inquiry-based education. They are the stuff of which memories are made.

The Great Brain inquiry process gives learners a different slant on education. Participants soon discover that:

- They are responsible for their own learning and behavior.

- Satisfying accomplishment is the result of personal effort.

- They are valuable, important people.

- Every person is gifted and talented.
- Cooperation with others is essential.
- Learning is a joyous activity.

The fourth pivotal principle for changing public education, *Invite Inquiry*, like the others, is the opposite of what public schools are normally organized to do. It is the opposite of force-feeding the state curriculum for 13 years of public schooling. Inviting Inquiry is a high form of respect for autonomy. It is another way to help children be responsible for their own learning. According to Postman and Weingartner, "it works you over in entirely different ways and generates a different, bolder, and more potent kind of intelligence."

My objective in sharing what follows is to help our society break free from a crippling tradition. What happens if we refocus education and *Invite Inquiry* as the basic mode of educational interaction with children over a prolonged period—all during a child's formative years, both in the home and in school? What are the advantages of nurturing a child's innate curiosity? How do we do it?

At Hill Field Elementary School and Whitesides School we found it makes a big difference in changing a child's attitudes toward school and learning even if s/he is given only a portion of the time for inquiry. Unfortunately, we were still tied to the state-mandated curriculum, but a partnership with parents and a focus on helping children grow in greatness gave teachers courage to put the state curriculum aside at least part of the time. With teachers' and parents' minds set on nurturing Identity, Inquiry, and Interaction, they invented several strategies that started to change the lives of children and themselves. Although I cannot show evidence from carefully controlled empirical studies, I know deep in my bones that some of the strategies helped children grow in feelings of self-worth, curiosity, kindness, and a different, deeper kind of knowing.

ૐ

How the Brain Works

If we were to really understand how the human brain works, I'm sure we would quickly change the way public schools function. Those who have engaged in an intensive study of the brain have been telling us for years that public schools don't operate in a way that's compatible with how human brains function. After reading some of the research studies I'm impressed with one major concept: Human brains learn helter-skelter. In other words, human brains have the natural ability to randomly gather thousands of pieces of information from the environment and connect these pieces with thousands of other pieces of information that are lying in one's mental storage—accumulated from many experiences—to build new personal concepts. Researchers have found that human learning may actually be suppressed by the way curriculum is organized and presented—in a linear fashion—in public schools. We have embraced the false notion that concepts must always be presented in a line, one after the other, for understanding to occur in a human mind. Scientists have found that what is logical and sequential for the teacher is probably not logical and sequential for any learner. Neve, Hart, and Thomas in a 1986 article in *Kappan* put it this way:

"Brain-compatible instruction dispenses with the hoary and ubiquitous notion that learning must occur in some arbitrary, sequential, "logical" order that has been officially sanctioned. Brain-based instruction stems from recognizing that the brain does not take logical steps down one path...but can go down a hundred different paths simultaneously (like an enormously powerful analogue computer). Random learning, like assembling a complex jigsaw puzzle, is seen as the way human brains work. This is aided by many varied experiences and by a global emphasis rather than by splintering learning into narrow subjects or units."

In order to understand why it is so important to *Invite Inquiry*, I have developed a model of how it seems to me the brain works. If you can visualize a mass, roughly the shape of a sphere, that is covered with thousands of tiny jig-saw puzzle-shaped pieces, each with a tiny fishing pole protruding outward, you will see my model of human brain function. Each of the miniature fishing poles—message receptors—is in constant motion casting a line to hook a piece of information that seems relevant to one's past experiences and reel it in.

Whenever the brain catches a piece of information through active, aggressive fishing (Inquiry), it is hauled inside and processed to become permanent personal knowledge. On the other hand, if information is imposed, rather than sought, it is plastered on the outside of the sphere where it soon is sloughed off and forgotten. Imposed learning is shallow and temporary, while learning gained from personal inquiry is deep and enduring.

There is a big difference between knowledge acquired from personal searching—finding answers to one's own questions—and unsolicited information. When Plato wrote that "knowledge acquired under compulsion obtains no hold on the mind," he was revealing a truth that scientists are only now beginning to understand. It is the reason why traditional education often fails to make as much of a difference as education that is based on personal inquiry.

Another metaphor for the brain could be a vacuum cleaner, or an aggressive octopus. When information is sucked into the brain and processed by one's free will, it has a much different effect on us than does unsolicited information. It is the reason why the fourth principle, *Invite Inquiry*, is so important and powerful. I like the way Victor Weisskopf, a prominent professor of physics, puts it:

People cannot learn by having information pressed into their brains. Knowledge has to be sucked into the brain, not pushed in. First, one must create a state of mind that craves knowledge, interest and wonder. You can teach only by creating an urge to know.

❧

INQUIRY-BASED HOMES AND SCHOOLS

A home or school organized for the purpose of helping the inhabitants become avid seekers after knowledge and wisdom is very different from those that are driven to impose a body of predetermined information. The first step in establishing the home or school as an inquiry center is to overcome a major mental block about curriculum. Some homes and many schools are tied to the false notion I mentioned in Chapter Three—that student achievement in curriculum is the major goal and purpose of education. This mindset leads to the creation of artificial, or contrived courses of study that are designed to standardize students.

The subject matter content most often found in textbooks and worksheets falls in this category. Once we understand the difference between genuine and artificial curriculum, we can proceed to organize homes and schools that are inquiry based.

Here is the difference: Genuine curriculum invites inquiry. It raises questions; it encourages investigation and digs deeper for connections between what is already in one's brain and the new material. Artificial curriculum, on the other hand, is usually found in textbooks and courses of study designed to produce a predetermined outcome or response. Remember Emerson's comment: "It is not for you to choose what he shall know, what he shall do."

Genuine content is the world and everything in it: people,

plants, animals, insects, birds, fish, rocks, mountains, rivers, sky, clouds—everything. It is the real stuff of our environment and is usually assimilated through our sense receptors. This is level one curriculum.

The second level of authentic curricula is to be found in such places as libraries, television, and on the World Wide Web. The material found in most library books is usually not written to produce a predetermined response in the reader; rather they are designed to offer information and to generate thought and questions.

When it becomes clear that the first three pivotal principles—Nurture Positive Diversity, Draw Forth Potential, and Respect Autonomy—are valid, we can get serious about the fourth—Invite Inquiry. The first teacher to catch the significance of this principle at Hill Field Elementary School was Jim Thurgood. When the school adopted Identity, Interaction, and Inquiry as its primary goals, Jim was the first to take visible action.

I relate his story to provide some clues as to some possible things you might do to establish an inquiry-based home or school. Most of all I'd like to pass on a philosophical attitude that seems to me makes the difference between authoritarian, imposed learning and learning that comes from personal seeking.

Jim Thurgood loves animals. He probably loves children even more. Over a period of several years of watching Mr. Thurgood teach fourth graders, I noticed that this remarkable teacher was fascinated with the magical effect that animals have on children. He always kept gerbils, hamsters, rabbits, reptiles—a variety of small animals and birds—in cages in his classroom. He found that children's problems—lack of love in the home, low confidence, or whatever—were always ameliorated when a child bonded with and cared for an animal. Jim showed children how to love and appreciate living things and the reciprocal benefits that come from this interaction. I thought of Mr. Thurgood as "Dr. Domuch" because of his uncanny ability to commune with animals and convey his amazing gift to children. Unfortunately, he retired early from teaching because of pressures to suppress his gifts in favor of delivering the state curriculum. Jim started a delightful pet store, *Teacher's Pets*, and continued to bless his community with his gifts.

When Human Greatness became the major goal and purpose of our school—with Inquiry as one of the three dimensions of greatness — Jim looked for a way to share his understanding of child/animal bonding with the whole school. One day he came to me and proposed that we replace the artificial plant area in the main entrance of the school with an aviary inquiry center.

The space he had in mind measured approximately four feet by fifteen and could be expanded to eight by fifteen by ten, floor to ceiling. It would be constructed with two by fours and chicken wire, and could be viewed from both sides as people entered the school from doors on either side.

Knowing full well that such a major change required permission from the Buildings and Grounds Department, Jim and I obtained the necessary materials and constructed an aviary in a few hours one evening under cover of darkness. We hoped to get forgiveness when building officials saw what a benefit this would be for the school. In the next few days Jim supplied the aviary with a variety of finches, canaries, parakeets, a real hibiscus tree, and birdhouses for nesting.

As you can imagine, the aviary became a big hit with children. There was always a crowd on both sides watching the birds. Teachers would soon learn how to take advantage of this interest and guide children into many interesting investigations. Actually, teachers were almost forced into it when it became difficult to pull children away from the aviary to return to their classrooms.

One day the Director of Buildings and Grounds, having heard of our innovation, came to see for himself what we had wrought. To our surprise, when he saw the fascinated observers lined up three deep watching the birds, he decided to replace our amateurish carpentry with an expertly designed and built aviary with two parts—one side for birds and the other side for small animals. In a few days it was completed with beautiful hardwood and heavy screening to take the place of our chicken wire and rough lumber.

We now had a deluxe miniature zoo/aviary. It became the featured inquiry center of several we developed at the school. During the next couple of years, Mr. Thurgood supplied the zoo with an interesting variety of birds and animals. Among these was a hen that made a nest, laid fertile eggs with the help of a feisty rooster, sat on them for the requisite 21 days and 5 hours, and brought forth a dozen delightful chicks.

Can you imagine the flood of questions that came from children involved in this experience? How does a hen make a baby chick with an egg? What does the rooster have to do with it? Just reading about it, doesn't this story elicit questions in your mind? Especially, how did the teachers handle the delicate sex questions? Children who grow up on farms usually learn about sex in a natural, wholesome way, while those who didn't, often develop unhealthy misconceptions. Jim's zoo became a fascinating inquiry center where children developed healthy attitudes toward the reproduction of species. All of the parakeets and finches multiplied exceedingly under the loving care of Jim Thurgood and his assistants (usually poor, neglected children).

Of the many temporary inhabitants of the zoo, and perhaps the favorite, was Panchita, a capuchin monkey, given to us by a missionary returning from Brazil. He had obtained Panchita when she was very young, raised her as a pet, and tearfully donated her to the Hill Field School Zoo when he found his life too busy to care for her anymore.

Panchita was a wonderful zoo attraction. She probably lived outside the zoo as much as she did in it. When Panchita learned how to turn the knob on the zoo door she would sometimes wander through the halls and unexpectedly drop in on a class to the screaming delight of children.

Everyone was sad on the day we donated Panchita to the Hogle Zoo in Salt Lake City. In return, we were able to have a large South American rodent, an agouti, on temporary loan from the Zoo. As time went on, our elementary school zoo hosted such things as baby goats, a strutting male turkey gobbler, and a large snake.

As an inquiry center, the Hill Field Elementary School Zoo was unexcelled. It stimulated children to ask many questions and go to the library to look for answers. It was also a place where children would sit and draw pictures of the animals and birds. It was a sad day for me when I learned, after my transfer to another school, that the zoo was torn out during the next summer while school was not in session. The school entrance returned to its former sterile appearance. It's very possible that the new principal succumbed to the pressure of school officials to deliver the no-nonsense, standardized curriculum.

There is no end to the ways you can make your school or home into an inquiry-based learning center. Here are some practical projects, from my own experience, that you might consider:

- We developed a library/media center where children and teachers could investigate printed and audiovisual materials. (If you can believe this—Hill Field Elementary School was a new school that was built without a library. During the summer we confiscated two adjoining class rooms and made a library.)

- We converted two small conference rooms next to the media center into a realia center and equipped it with real things from nature—rocks, seashells, bird nests, beehives, pine cones, insect collections, etc.—and investigation devices such as binoculars, magnifying lenses, telescopes, and microscopes that children and teachers could check out and use. We also obtained some war surplus, metal 30 mm ammunition boxes, and invited parents, children, and teachers to make inquiry boxes. Typical of these boxes was one that contained some electric wire, batteries, bulbs, switches, a large nail, a small compass, and an inquiry guide for learning about electric currents.

- With the help of parents, we made a map of all interesting inquiry sites within a two-, five-, and ten-mile radius of the school. These were used for numerous walking and transported field trips. They could pay at least part of the expenses.

- We tore apart National Geographics magazines, and science books and rebound them into individual inquiry study units on a great variety of topics.

- We built a 50-gallon aquarium, stocked it with sea creatures, and obtained some war surplus 5-gallon glass jugs that we used to study leeches and other interesting water creatures.

- We converted two more adjacent classrooms that had a sliding partition and again, with the help of war-surplus materials, organized an elementary shop/arts and crafts center.

These are just a few of the creative actions that arose out of a community that embraced a different, inquiry-based philosophy of education. Now I want to tell you about another school that was on the verge of greatness until it was overcome with the philosophy and pressures of standardization.

I tell the following story with the anticipation that you will get inspiration to refocus your own school or home.

⁂

THE DREAM SCHOOL

Several years ago I met a couple of unusual elementary teachers at the home of my friend, Arnie Langberg. As you may recall, he was the man who organized a high school after the Walkabout pattern of freedom and responsibility. One of these teachers, Cyndi Dieken, had heard about my work and asked Arnie if a meeting could be arranged. To make a long story short, I spent an afternoon with Arnie and two delightful ladies talking about what an elementary school could be like if teachers were given freedom to pursue their dreams for children. After a wonderful afternoon of fantasizing, I gave Cyndi and her friend copies of my first book, *Redesigning Education,* and they left.

Some years went by. I had almost forgotten the meeting when the phone rang at my home. Cyndi was on the line to tell about their efforts to incorporate the Education for Greatness philosophy at the Lab School in Fort Collins, Colorado. Things were not going as well as she hoped and Cyndi was calling to ask if I could come and talk to the teachers. They could pay at least part of the expenses.

I went to Fort Collins and spent a pleasant afternoon talking with eight teachers who seemed eager to improve education at the Lab School. These folks seemed to be in an ideal situation: an old building designed for twice as many classrooms, but with only eight classes of about 25 each. Furthermore, they had applied for charter status for a school that was already expected to innovate and try new ideas. In the evening I met with teachers and parents together and

113

found that parents were very receptive to the Education for Greatness philosophy. Earlier in the day I had found, when I visited several classes, that there were numerous parents in the school helping in many ways. It looked like Cyndi and her colleague had laid the groundwork for important changes. Promising to keep in touch, I left the next day to return home.

I met with the staff of the Lab School on two more occasions. The last time is indelibly printed in my memory. During the meeting, with a focus on student inquiry, one of the teachers said, "Let's organize our school with eight inquiry centers, each built around the gifts, talents, and interests of our teachers. Students could then rotate or move freely from center to center to find personal quests." This seemed to strike a chord and teachers immediately started to choose centers. One of them, the only man on the staff, said, "I'll make a science and math inquiry center." Another said, "I'd like to organize a quiet place where we feature the reading and writing of books and stories." A third said, "I'll organize a little theater where children can write and act out their own plays, design costumes, and make scenery." Another said, "Let me be in charge of a shop/art room where children can come to design, create, and make things with all kinds of materials." Another said, "I'd like to do a nature center filled with living plants, animals and rocks—with a door to the outside so children can go on guided excursions." It went on until all had indicated a special interest.

Can you imagine how I felt? Like I was in the delivery room when someone was giving birth to a new baby! That same evening the parents came to a meeting and one of the teachers enthusiastically presented the plan for a school built around inquiry centers. Her presentation was greeted with applause and cheers. Parents were excited about the possibilities.

This occurred in the spring, just before school let out for the year. During the summer I had visions of parents and children joining hands to create eight fascinating inquiry centers at the Lab School. I could see each one in my mind's eye and communicated with Cyndi about the opportunities that were theirs to involve parents and children in the creation and operation of each inquiry center.

I wish I could report on the realization of a wonderful dream. Alas, the Lab School Community did not transform the school into an exciting inquiry-based learning center. The tidal wave of standardization engulfed the school and drowned the dreams of parents and teachers alike. My vision of an ideal, dream school was washed away in the flood.

This was also the spring that the Poudre River overflowed its banks and flooded a large area of Fort Collins. The flood became a catastrophic metaphor for a dark system of education that is now chest-deep and rising by the hour. Fortunately, floodwaters did not reach the school, but perhaps worse, teachers and parents were overcome by politicians' mania for standardization.

Cyndi was devastated by the news that her beloved school would not be allowed to meet the curious urges of children. It would have to buckle under to the needs of politicians. Rather than compromise her integrity, Cindy quit her job at the Lab School and started a new venture.

ॐ

Curious Parents and Teachers
Curious Children

An inquiry-based philosophy of teaching has radical implications for homes and schools. Some of us will need to make a major mental habit adjustment in the way we perceive the world. It presents an exciting opportunity to learn to see with fresh eyes. To actuate the fourth principle, *Invite Inquiry,* some of us will need to go back to our early childhood and retrieve something the public school system stole from us bit by bit, our curiosity. I call it the Great Brain Robbery because the public school system unintentionally, in an effort to make us smart, in an effort to *give* us knowledge, did just the opposite. It robbed each of us of a curious attitude and the chance to acquire personal knowledge, the knowledge that comes from mentally processing new information so that it becomes our own, not knowledge adopted from others.

It is interesting to observe the robbery while it's taking place. As children enter kindergarten they are usually full of questions, unless, as happens in rare cases, curiosity is squelched in the home before a child comes to school. As children move up through the grades it's easy to observe a gradual decline in the amount and quality of children's questions.

The official core curriculum has become so pervasive that there is little room for questions that may lead into a thousand paths. You've probably heard of scientists' claims that most of us are using only five to ten percent of our mental capacities. What if we could increase this to over 95 percent? What would children grow up to be like if the knowledge they acquired in schools and homes was the kind that came from personal inquiry? What would they be like if their information fishing poles had more chances to catch bigger fish and convert them into dynamic brain and body cells? What would it be like, if most of the information obtained in schools and homes did not slough off the brain, but was internalized to become a vital part of children for them to remember and use throughout their lives? What would happen if a child's power to ask penetrating questions was nurtured to increase each year?

The fourth pivotal principle, *Invite Inquiry*, in some respects is already in place—put there by our creator and supported by a rich, stimulating environment. Humans have been blessed with a curious nature and placed in a world full of wonderful things. Our challenge is not to spoil it all by force-feeding artificial, contrived information into delicate hearts and minds.

I've already described some physical environments that can be organized to invite student inquiry. Now I want to talk about the human element.

❧

THE POWER OF EXAMPLE

Perhaps the most stimulating strategy for inviting inquiry is for parents and teachers to stop thinking of themselves as information dispensers and become active, seeking learners. The most powerful teaching strategy I know is for a parent or professional teacher to take an intense interest in a child and learn from him. This strategy calls for a reversal of roles, for the child to be the teacher and the teacher to be the learner.

Being curious is part of human nature. All we have to do is revive a gift that has atrophied from lack of use. If we have forgotten how to be curious or have had our inquiry stolen from us, we may have to return to a childish way of looking at things and find joy and wonder in everything about us. With conscious effort we can renew and expand the curious attitude we were born with. As parents and teachers, we can best invite inquiry by being examples of curiosity for children.

What message is conveyed when children see *us* being curious? When children observe the important people in their lives being hungry for knowledge, showing an insatiable curiosity, and a zest for learning, what does it tell them? If a teacher, whether parent or professional, is first and foremost a learner, it conveys the message that learning is enjoyable and important.

In sharp contrast, what message do children get when they see someone who knows all the answers and is obsessed with showing it? After many years of watching teachers I'm impressed with the difference between two teaching styles and the effect these styles have on children. On the one hand, there are those who know their subject and sincerely have a strong desire to teach their knowledge to others. Many of these teachers are very skilled at making their subject interesting for children. They plaster knowledge on the brains of their learners so deftly that some of it is taken in and internalized for long-term use. In current terminology these teachers are said to be using the direct teaching method.

There is a growing body of adherents for this method. These people often hold up student growth in standardized achievement test scores to substantiate their claim for the benefits of direct teaching.

There's another, much smaller, group of teachers who give the impression that they know their subject, but are just as interested in learning more about their subject as they are in teaching what they know. It could be said that these teachers are just as interested in helping learners find out what they, the teachers, don't know as they are in delivering the knowledge they already possess. These teachers could be said to be using the inquiry method. They invite student questions and often say, "I don't know. Let's find out together." These teachers don't hold up standardized achievement scores as evidence of student growth, largely because these tests don't fit the creative, deep learning that happens with the inquiry method.

The word *creative,* as used here, describes two things that happen when a learner pulls in some information by personally seeking it out. First, the learner creates his or her own knowledge by making mental connections between the new information and other self-constructed knowledge already filed in the brain. It could be said that this new personal knowledge is filed in the dynamic file for long-term availability, to be used in solving a problem or in some other beneficial way. This is the second creative act. In other words, knowledge obtained from personal inquiry is self-constructed and then used for some future purpose that is unique to the user.

I vividly remember children who would learn spelling words to pass the test on Friday and misspell them in a written composition the next week. On the other hand, children would retain the spelling of words they needed in writing that was important to them.

There are other, more subtle differences between the direct teaching method and the inquiry method, which, I believe, account for the differences in student learning. With direct instruction the curriculum is closed. There is a boundary line around the content that was placed there by those who wrote the text with the goal of producing a predetermined response in the learner. With the inquiry method, the curriculum is open. There is no limiting line around the content. The subject, be it math, science, art, geography, or whatever, merges over into other content areas, ever expanding. There is no intention to produce a predetermined response in the learner other than a flood of questions and creative use of the knowledge obtained through personal inquiry. The result of this kind of learning is often surprising. Standardized achievement tests are useless for measuring student growth from personal inquiry for several reasons:

- The learning is unexpected and unpredictable.

- Personal, creative knowing is deeper and more intense, and affects each child in countless, immeasurable ways.

- It's nigh impossible to devise test questions to ascertain how a learner sees new relationships between various disciplines or subjects.

There's one final thing I'd like to say about standardized achievement testing. Because of the limitations expressed above, these tests automatically call for direct instruction, a method that usually results in shallow learning, mainly because the learner has little personal involvement in the information that is being supplied. The tests call for uniformity and severely limit the amount of time teachers can allow for student self-initiated inquiry. They work against children who want to build their own knowledge through the processes of personal inquiry.

※

SEARCHING FOR QUESTIONS

Before moving into the next chapter to talk about the professionalization of teaching, I'd like to mention another aspect of *Inviting Inquiry*. The number one tool for inquiry is the power to ask good questions. There are many ways to regain what was lost or stolen from us. I've already implied that we can develop a curious attitude by looking at everything with fresh eyes, as a child, to see what makes it tick.

I'm reminded of a classic case of curiosity deprivation. One day, a few years ago, my wife and I were standing, holding hands, on the edge of the north rim of the Grand Canyon. It was one of those days of perfect temperature, sunshine, and a cool breeze. We were awestruck with the beauty of everything, the cumulus-laden sky, the gnarled pines, the spring flowers, a soaring eagle, and especially the immense, multicolored chasm at our feet. The mighty Colorado River was a shimmering ribbon and barely audible, whenever the wind was right, almost a mile straight down. We were totally spellbound with the grandeur of it all. We were alone in a glorious moment with our Creator. The silence was awesome.

After a while of being speechlessly entranced, we heard footsteps behind us. We turned to see a man and a woman approaching on the path. They came up beside us and the man, after a quick perusal, said to his partner, "What a hell of a hole. Let's go." And they turned around and left.

I was stunned. Here we were, standing at the edge of eternity, on the brink of one of the most beautiful places on earth, when we were suddenly assaulted with perhaps the most extreme case of insensitivity I've ever experienced. How could two people, with all their senses seemingly intact, not feel what my wife and I were feeling? Did they not see what we saw? Why did they not linger and feast upon this magnificent scene? To this day, many years later, I'm still curious as to the motives behind such strange behavior. When we returned to the parking lot, we found the couple had left some trash from their fast-food meal lying on the ground.

What can we do to prevent the loss of curiosity and wonder in children? We can start by asking questions. A person full of curiosity and wonder about the world is a person full of questions. A parent, or other teacher, who wants to be an example of curiosity will ask many questions about everything, always searching for the best questions to ask.

It's been said that it is more important and useful to look for good questions than it is to look for good answers. Why? Because insightful questions will usually lead to other, more penetrating ways of seeking. A little question is often swallowed up by a bigger question, which in turn, is swallowed up by a larger one—and on and on, until we catch a whale.

The more we know, the more we realize how much we don't know. I invite readers to find ways to get in the habit of personal inquiry so that you may become an example of curiosity for children. Look for questions everywhere and you'll soon find a new zest for life, a passion for learning that will rub off on everyone. We can best Invite Inquiry by showing how much fun it is. We *can* change our attitudes and habits of perceiving the world. I used a story from Marion Hanks's *The Gift of Self* that illustrates this kind of change in my first book, *Redesigning Education*. It bears repeating here because it is such a good example of what can happen when we change our way of looking at the world:

"An obscure spinster woman insisted that she never had a chance. She muttered these words to Dr. Louis Aggassiz, a distinguished naturalist, after one of his lectures in London. In response to her complaint, he replied, "Do you say, madam, you never had a chance? What do you do?"

"I am single and help my sister run a boarding house."

"What do you do?" he asked again.

"I skin potatoes and chop onions."

He said, "Madam, where do you sit during these interesting but homely duties?"

"On the bottom step of the kitchen stairs."

"Where do your feet rest?"

"On the glazed brick."

"What is glazed brick?"

"I don't know, sir."

"How long have you been sitting there?"

She said, "Fifteen years."

"Madam, here is my personal card," said Dr. Agassiz. "Would you kindly write me a letter concerning the nature of a glazed brick?"

She went home and explored the dictionary and discovered that a brick was a piece of baked clay. That definition seemed too simple to send to Dr. Agassiz, so after the dishes were washed, she went to the library and in an encyclopedia read that glazed brick is vitrified kaolin and hydrous aluminum silicate. She didn't know what that meant, but she was curious to find out. She took the word *vitrified* and read all she could about it. Then she visited museums. She moved out of the basement of her life and into a new world on the wings of vitrified. And having started, she took the word *hydrous*, studied geology, and went back in her studies to a time when the world was covered with clay beds.

One afternoon she went to a brickyard, where she found out about the history of more than 120 kinds of bricks and tiles and why there have to be so many. She sat down and wrote thirty-six pages on the subject of glazed brick and tile.

Back came a letter from Dr. Agassiz:

"Dear Madam, this is the best article I have ever seen on the subject. If you will kindly change the three words marked with asterisks, I will have it published and pay you for it."

A short time later there came a letter that brought $250, and penciled at the bottom of the letter was this query:

"What was under those bricks?"

She had learned the value of time and answered with a single word: "Ants."

He wrote back and said, "Tell me about the ants."

She began to study ants. She found there were between eighteen hundred and twenty five hundred different kinds. There are ants so tiny you could put three head-to-head on a pin and have standing room left over for other ants; ants an inch long that march in solid armies half a mile wide, driving everything ahead of them; ants that are blind; ants that get wings on the afternoon of the day they die; ants that build anthills so tiny that you can cover one with a silver thimble; peasant ants that keep cows to milk and that then deliver the fresh milk to other ants in the colony.

After much reading, microscopic work, and deep study, the spinster sat down and wrote Dr. Agassiz 360 pages on the subject. He published the book and sent her the money, and using her earnings, she went to visit all the lands she had dreams of visiting."

This story shows what can happen when a caring person knows how to Invite Inquiry. Dr. Agassiz knew how to *Invite Inquiry* by making people aware of the knowledge that's available in ordinary, commonplace things we often take for granted. All around us there are wonderful discoveries to be made. We can *Invite Inquiry* by first doing it with ourselves. We can restore curiosity as a learning way of life. A curious attitude is contagious because it's so much fun. Others will see our newfound zest for life and want to join the party.

With inquiry education it's time to abandon an obsolete concept: homework. It was a tragic mistake to ever call the learning children do at home, *work*. This term has instilled in many generations the idea that learning is often miserable and undesirable. When we adopt *Invite Inquiry* as a principle for changing education, we automatically embrace a new concept: *Home Study*. This means that children can learn at home without being required or assigned to do it. The Great Brain Project and other strategies usually create the kind of interest that results in children wanting to do projects and learn wherever they are.

~

LITERACY THROUGH INQUIRY
INQUIRY THROUGH LITERACY

The library of my youth was a box of comic books on the front porch of a nearby neighbor. I remember making many visits to this library to exchange a Superman, Batman, or Dick Tracy comic for a new one whenever I needed another adventure. The supply was endless and ever-changing because all the kids in the neighborhood kept the comic book library fresh with new books they had traded for old ones. It was an honor system that worked a magic spell on all of us, and it resulted in a group of youngsters becoming voracious readers. The printed word, always linked with an action picture, made reading a most exciting adventure. I learned how to read through personal inquiry, the same way everyone learns how to read. It's a different inquiry process for every person because we are unique individuals. We have unique sensory receptors and unique backgrounds of experiences to connect us to the printed word. Like learning a language, reading is more *caught* than *taught*.

How do we learn to speak the language of our culture? We learn by being spoken to, over and over, and by watching the gestures of the speaker. Researchers have found that this is the best way to learn a foreign language as well. I have three grandchildren who learned how to speak and write Japanese while they were enrolled in a Japanese elementary school when their father was transferred to Japan on a business assignment for three years.

Learning to speak a language is a very complex process inside the brain that we may never fully understand. One thing we do know is that the process is personal and individual; it is different for every person. From this, and from many research studies, we can infer that the process of learning to read is also a result of personal, individual inquiry. Both learning to speak and learning to read are skills a person attains through self-directed learning. We do not formally teach talking, so why do we often make the mistake of trying to formally teach reading? If we understand the informal, natural way a child learns to speak the language of the culture, how does this help us know how to help children learn how to read? Should all children learn how to read at the same time? Just as there are individual rates for learning how to talk and walk, so also there are different rates for children learning how to read. Human beings are designed to be diverse!

Unfortunately, over time, some self-styled experts and textbook publishers have foisted artificial methods for teaching reading on schools. The textbook industry has reaped a fortune selling basic readers so children can be divided into slow, middle, and fast reading groups for direct instruction.

During my classroom teaching years I soon became very uncomfortable trying to teach reading the way supervisors wanted—with a basic reader and children divided by ability into three groups. I found that the read-around-in-a-circle kind of instruction was not for me. I got better results when I provided children with a great variety of reading materials from which they could choose and gave them plenty of time for silent reading. After silent reading, we often took time for students to share their excitement of the wonderful stories they were discovering. I'll never forget one day, while all the children were quietly reading, I heard a sobbing and looked up to see a little girl crying. When I went over to ask, "What's the matter?" Julie told me she had just finished *Biography of a Grizzly* by Earnest Thompson Seaton, and was distressed when Wob, the grizzly hero ended his long life by walking into the valley of death. Julie had lost a true friend! Later, when Julie shared this experience with the class, several children formed a waiting list to read this classic story.

Sometimes we ran out of time for children to share their reading experiences, so we created a file so students could write about their reading on a 4 x 6 card. Students used this file to share their feelings about a book as well as to find other books to read. One year I decided to measure and compare the difference between my previously used reading group method and my new method of surrounding children with high-quality literature and giving them time for reading and sharing their experiences with books.

When I compared the results on reading tests, I was surprised at the difference. With the old, reading-group method of using controlled-vocabulary basic readers, my fifth graders advanced the expected one year of growth. The next year, when I immersed children in a variety of great literature and provided time for silent reading, students averaged three years of growth in one year!

Later, as the principal of two schools that decided to nurture the three dimensions of greatness, I learned more valuable lessons about human literacy. One of the teachers, Beth Moore, was very successful using an unusual approach. While teaching first graders, she obtained a large-print typewriter and used it to transcribe children's stories as they described the pictures they made with art materials. At first, these stories were short and simple ("This is my dog.") and over time, became more elaborate ("This is a picture of our family camping at Bear Lake."). The stories were attached to the bottom of the picture, then pinned up for display in the classroom. At the end of the day, each child took the illustrated story home to read to parents.

How does this kind of reading instruction compare with the Dick and-Jane, read-around-in-a-group, kind of instruction that many of us were exposed to? Do you see the difference? Beth Moore provided each child with instant success in reading because students were reading their own precious words. At the same time, children were developing their creative power with art materials. Students also learned how to read each other's stories.

֍

The School Post Office

When the teachers at Whitesides Elementary School made a commitment to help children grow in the second dimension of greatness, Interaction, they discovered an amazing tool. One day, three fourth-graders came to my office and asked if they could make an announcement to the school over the public address system. When I asked, "What for?" they responded, "We want to start a school post office. We've made a mailbox and will invite everyone in the school to write letters to others in the school and drop them in the mailbox. Each day we will deliver the letters to the ones they are addressed to, if the letters have the right room numbers on them. We especially invite cooks, custodians, librarians, parents, secretaries, everyone, and even you, the principal, to write letters."

When I gave permission for the announcement, I had no idea what a commotion it would cause. Nor did I realize that an important discovery was about to be made about human literacy. The announcement was made and a large official-looking mailbox was placed in the hallway outside the office door. Then the fun began. It was but minutes until the first letter arrived.

The post office made a dramatic impact on the life of the school. Within a day or two of its inauguration, some other school activities had to be curtailed or postponed in order to provide students with the time they needed for writing. The flood of mail was so great that the teacher, Della Russell, and her students who started the project, had to reorganize their room into a mail-processing center. Some adult staff members, including me, received so many letters we became concerned about how we would ever have time to reply. Children started writing letters at home and rushing to school each day to read their mail.

Other problems began to emerge as a few students started to write hateful notes and send them to others whom they disliked. This was partially solved when teachers pointed out that letter writers would usually respond in kind: If you want to receive an interesting, uplifting letter, that is the kind you should write. If you want to receive a letter that builds your self-esteem (Identity), kindness and friendship (Interaction), or stimulates intellectual activity (Inquiry), that is the kind you should write. Children were encouraged to write, not only to their close friends, but to someone whom they felt needed a friend.

The school post office became a valuable device for building Interaction attitudes and skills. Many children started to write as never before without being assigned or coaxed into doing so. The post office made it possible for students to pass notes without getting in trouble. They learned how to spell new words at a rapid rate. Many kindergarten and first graders began reading and writing without formal instruction. There was powerful motivation when these children received personal letters and needed to answer them. The teachers invited older students to write to younger ones in clear manuscript printing, instead of cursive, to facilitate this process.

Children soon found the importance of learning how to address their handmade envelopes properly and of putting a return address on their mail. They also learned the necessity of writing legibly. The school post office also became a valuable instrument for nurturing Inquiry as students sought help with vocabulary, spelling, and grammar.

After about a week, post office fever subsided somewhat as some children concentrated on the quality of their letter writing rather than quantity. Many children started to expand their contacts to include pen pals in other states and other countries. The teachers decided to keep the post office as a permanent part of the school and rotate the sorting and delivery jobs among the classes. Some classes made trips to the local post office to learn how to operate a mail delivery system.

The school post office is a strategy that is compatible with how the brain works and learns. It involves a flood of randomly supplied information, personal inquiry, and learning by doing. Perhaps most importantly, it is an activity that generates its own steam. Students do not need to be coaxed, assigned, or required to participate.

Brain research is now telling us that the best way to help children learn the skills of communication—listening, speaking, reading, and writing—is to immerse a child in a pleasant, interactive environment where he or she has as many opportunities as possible to actually practice these skills. Just as a child can't learn to ride a bicycle until s/he gets on and starts pedaling and balancing, neither can a child learn to communicate until s/he engages in real communication. A child learns to read by reading, to write by writing, to listen by listening, and to speak by speaking. The brain picks up the cues it needs while it is engaged in the process.

This means that we need to drastically reduce the amount of time we spend *teaching* literacy and start having children spend more time *doing* literary things. The important thing to remember in teaching listening, speaking, reading, and writing is that literacy is not the goal; it is a means of helping children grow in three dimensions of greatness.

Literacy acquired without nurturing self-worth (Identity), respectful communication (Interaction), and curiosity (Inquiry) is misguided at best and may be harmful to the recipient. If we build literacy with this in mind, we will usually avoid doing things that dampen children's natural curiosity and hunger for knowledge. If you want more information on helping children learn how to read in the natural way, I recommend three books: *Unspeakable Acts, Unnatural Practices: Flaws and*

Fallacies in Scientific Reading Instruction by Frank Smith, *The Power of Reading: Insights from the Research* by Stephan Krashen and *Beyond Traditional Phonics* by Margaret Moustafa.

The fourth principle for changing the direction of public education, *Invite Inquiry*, is a vital principle that will necessitate a major attitudinal change on the part of many parents, teachers, and especially some influential politicians and business leaders. My experience tells me that it will be well worth the effort to accommodate this principle. While direct teaching is sometimes much easier than inviting inquiry, the results are entirely different: the first is shallow and temporary, the second endures endlessly.

CHAPTER 9

The Fifth Principle:
Support Professionalism

There is no word in the language that I revere more than "teacher." None. My heart sings when a kid refers to me as his teacher, and it always has. I've honored myself and the entire family of man by becoming a teacher. —Pat Conroy

Whack! A sharp blow to the top of my head was instantaneously followed by the sound of breaking glass—followed by deathly silence. My classmates were staring at me, wondering what I had done to merit such treatment from our teacher. Most of them had seen C. J. Manning throw the hard-backed eraser that bounced off my head and crashed through the window at the back of the classroom.

I knew immediately what I'd done to deserve the missile attack. I had been leaning across the aisle between our desks whispering with June Hadley, a cute girl who had caught my fancy. We all knew that verbal interaction with others was rarely tolerated in Mr. Manning's classroom. Most often he would throw a piece of chalk whenever students were caught talking. This time C. J. felt the infraction called for larger caliber ammunition.

Clarence Manning was a portly, older man, always dressed in a gray suit with a vest, complete with gold pocket watch and chain. He limped with a cane and, over the years, had compensated for a physical handicap by learning how to throw things with great accuracy. He taught fourth and fifth graders in a two-room school in our small town in rural Utah.

I still revere Clarence Manning as one of my greatest teachers. After many years, he still stands at the front of a long line of teachers who influenced my life. I'll never forget his emotional rendition of Longfellow's *Evangeline*. Every day after lunch he would read to us, sometimes with tears in his eyes and a choke in his throat.

It may seem strange that a person would hold in high esteem a teacher who throws things at his students. These days this kind of teaching behavior would not be tolerated. A long time ago teachers were so honored and respected that people would not question a teacher's behavior. I did not tell my parents of the eraser incident until long after it occurred, but I doubt they would have spoken to Mr. Manning about it anyhow. They would have felt I got what I deserved.

Nearly all of my teachers were dedicated professionals who practiced their art with love and great skill. In those days teachers were held up by society with honor and respect. As I began my professional teaching career in 1950, I looked forward to becoming part of this elite group.

Everything went well early in my career. My community did, in fact, treat me with kind deference, but with the proliferation of standardized achievement tests and talk of accountability, conditions gradually started to change for me and other teachers as well. We would soon no longer be regarded as competent professionals. Why? Mainly because we could not produce the uniform product that legislators and business executives were demanding. The harder we tried to shape students into a standard mold, the worse it got.

There was great pressure to ignore student individuality and do what was expected: make sure all students were able to know and do the same things. This resulted in a rapid decline in student cooperation and discipline, which called for more "rigor," a favorite word of politicians and business executives, and a call for "higher standards." When students rebelled at being treated as products on an assembly line, teachers took the blame and were asked to double their efforts to standardize students and apply extreme disciplinary measures. As more testing was called for, conditions gradually worsened until in 2002 Congress passed the President's education bill that allocated federal money and assistance according to achievement test results. The President and his consortium of experts wheeled out a new motto, "No Child Left Behind," a catchy phrase that removed the last vestiges of freedom for children and their teachers.

Teachers, students, and parents have all been victims of misguided but well-meaning efforts to improve education. They are caught in a vortex of degradation. The scenario goes like this: (1) Politicians begin to use standardized testing to hold teachers accountable. (2) Teachers respond with direct instruction unsolicited by students. (3) Personal inquiry decreases. (4) Student apathy, discipline problems, and dropouts increase. (5) Test scores decline. (6) Legislators call for more rigor, higher standards, and more testing. (7) A standardized, teacher-proof curriculum is developed. (8) Creative teaching disappears as teachers dutifully follow the new manuals. (9) Many teachers are demoralized and leave the profession. (10) Test scores decline again. (11) Student apathy and discipline problems increase again.

Will our society have enough sense to put an end to this frightening scenario? There is a way out of this thorny dilemma: *Support Professionalism*. The fifth principle for changing education—*Support Professionalism*—is to restore teaching to its time-honored place in our society. It may be the most powerful and effective way to reverse the trend and put education back on track to true reform. By holding teachers accountable for doing things that are possible, instead of holding them accountable for doing the impossible task of standardizing children, we can restore the teaching profession to a position of trust and respect, mainly because the results will be vastly different. As parents we can also hold ourselves accountable for doing what great parents have always done. We can act as professional teachers in our homes.

The fifth principle for redesigning education, *Support Professionalism*, is the doorway to Mission Possible. It will come from a major cultural attitude change that embraces the principles of this book. It *is* possible for us to value and nurture Positive Human Diversity. It *is* possible to Draw Forth the Latent Potential of Learners. It *is* possible for us to Respect Student Autonomy. It *is* entirely possible and relatively easy to Invite Personal Inquiry. Of course, all of this is easier said than done, but now there's new hope. There's much reason to believe that significant changes are finally possible.

I've just finished reading a great little book that supports and adds another dimension to my contention that tradition prevents changes in education: *The Teaching Gap* by James Stigler and James Hiebert. These authors tell about a major study that was conducted to find out why American students lag so far behind those in other countries in mathematics, especially those in Japan.

The study began with video photographers, a native of each of three countries, Germany, Japan, and the United States, going to a different classroom each day for seven months and videotaping eighth grade teachers teaching a mathematics lesson. When the videotaping was completed, a team of researchers and math teachers from each country assembled at UCLA to study the tapes. They engaged in a complicated process of analysis that took several months.

Their conclusion was a complete affirmation of my belief that tradition is a ruling force. These researchers, after many hours of study, reflection, and discussion, agreed that teaching, in each of the countries studied, is primarily shaped by the culture. In other words, we all assimilate basic teaching methods from those who taught us for twelve or more years. That's why nearly everyone is a professed expert on teaching. It's the reason politicians, lawyers, business executives, farmers, everyone, consider themselves to be teaching authorities. It's also the reason why it's so difficult to change people's vision of teaching. Not only is it tradition, but it's also a lifestyle custom of a proud people.

To illustrate this, let me relate an example of how teachers teach a mathematics concept in the USA with how it is done in Japan. In the United States, teachers typically show students, often on an overhead projector, how to do a mathematical process such as how to add unlike fractions (1/3 + 1/4). Following the teacher's demonstration, the students are assigned to do many similar problems for practice until they master the process.

In Japan, the problem of the day is presented and students are challenged to figure out, individually or in small groups, how to solve the problem. This is followed by much discussion and demonstration of the thinking process of various students and recorded on the chalkboard. Several avenues to a solution are explored. Students are not expected to do many problems for practice. Teachers in Japan use the chalkboard rather than overhead projectors because the chalkboard is more suitable for recording the linear "story" of student's thought processes as they explore various avenues for solving the daily problem.

The Japanese system is more closely related to what I call an inquiry method of teaching. Less student practice is needed because students have been guided to integrate their own knowledge, a process that builds understanding. The American system is usually direct instruction. Knowledge is plastered on the outside of the brain and soon sloughs off. The German method fits in between these two. These differences may explain why Japanese students perform so much better on tests. When Japanese students are presented with a problem on a test, they have learned how to figure out a solution, on the spot, even if they have never seen a similar problem. American students, on the other hand, deficient in inquiry skills, must rely on memory of a process that matches the problem. If it so happens that the test produces a problem that has never been encountered by the student, or the student has forgotten the process, s/he will probably not be able to arrive at a solution.

The approaches of teachers in the three countries were so consistently applied by many teachers that the researchers were forced to conclude that teaching is a cultural activity. It is a system learned over a long period of time while sitting in public and private school classrooms. While each teacher exhibited a unique teaching style, it was always consistent within the overall cultural mode.

This brings us to an interesting point. The American system of teaching is basically an information delivery system that is deeply ingrained in the heads of most people in our culture. The factory conveyor belt is often used as a metaphor for schooling in our country because of the prevalent practice of teachers conveying information to students. When we think of teaching we most often think of a teacher explaining, expounding knowledge, or showing students how to do something. The postal system with teachers as mail carriers could also be an apt symbol of teaching in the United States.

These visions of teaching may be a major reason why so many efforts to improve education have failed. We keep asking teachers to improve the delivery system, the only system we know. We keep asking teachers to improve the way they plaster information on the outside of children's brains. Teachers have actually been asked to try harder and harder to do the wrong things better and better!

We are now discovering that students do not retain unsought knowledge that is conveyed or delivered to them. They learn best from personal inquiry, by pursuing information on their own initiative to build their own knowledge. A shopping mall is a better metaphor for what happens when students go searching for the information they need to fill in the blanks they perceive in their own knowledge.

In our country we have spent millions of dollars and countless hours of energy trying to perfect a system of education that doesn't work very well. We have exhausted nearly every possible way of improving the conveyor belt when all the while we should have been working to improve the shopping mall!

Another example of our cultural mindset about teaching is found in the way teachers most often convey a major concept in geology. Following textbooks written by experts in the field, they teach that rocks are classified in three major categories: igneous, metamorphic, and sedimentary. Pictures of rocks thus classified, or real rocks, are then shown to support the concept. Students are often asked to examine a rock and tell in which category it fits.

Now contrast this with an inquiry method in which students are given a variety of small rocks and are challenged to see how many different classifications they can produce. Working as individuals, or in small groups, students will produce an interesting variety of categories for classifying their rocks—by shape, size, color, hardness, composition, texture, weight, and more. As part of this exercise students can be challenged to arrange their rocks from lightest to heaviest and prove their arrangement by inventing their own weight-measuring devices. Commercially made measuring tools are not allowed until afterwards to check and compare the results of student's arrangements.

It is fascinating to watch students invent ways to measure the weight of their rocks. If the rocks contain enough variety, I have found that sometimes students will develop theories about density and mass and show why a large, porous rock sometimes weighs less than a smaller one. In one of my workshops, students decided to demonstrate this concept by immersing the rocks in water and measuring the amount of liquid displaced by each rock.

The value of engaging students in hands-on inquiry should be obvious. Students can learn much more about the classification of rocks, or anything else, through observing, weighing, measuring, and comparing objects and events than they can by being told what conclusions they should draw from their experiences. After students have had their own experiences classifying rocks, the categories, igneous, metamorphic, and sedimentary have much more meaning for them.

⅋

A Different Cultural Vision

How do we go about changing a culture to reflect a different vision of teaching? What can we do to break a well-established pattern? How can we overcome a deeply entrenched tradition? The vision of teaching I have tried to convey in this book is much different from the one that is often displayed in our culture. Supporting Professionalism in the context of this book does not mean supporting business as usual in schools and in many homes. *Supporting Professionalism* means that we will support a new kind of teaching—the kind that follows the six pivotal principles Let's now examine some of the implications of *Supporting Professionalism* as defined by the principles.

※

VALUE AND NURTURE POSITIVE
HUMAN DIVERSITY

How do we support schoolteachers and ourselves in attempts to nurture positive differences? We must somehow come to an agreement that building positive human diversity is a valid, exciting mission for schools and homes. I will suggest some ways to convey to teachers that it's now okay to treat children as individuals and support them in doing so.

It's not only possible, but highly desirable to hold teachers responsible for treating each child as a unique person. Nearly all teachers will welcome the chance to prove they can value and nurture positive human diversity. What a relief it will be for teachers to have the standardization monkey lifted off their backs and replaced with an invitation to be professional teachers! Albert Einstein is reported to have said: "I believe in standardizing automobiles, not human beings."

What an invigorating stimulus it will be for teachers to be freed from the education assembly line—freed from being treated as subordinate workers taking orders from people who are far removed from classrooms and who know very little about teaching. To be treated as a competent professional will breathe new life, zest, and enthusiasm into every teacher.

Restoring dignity to the teaching profession is no more complicated than for lawmakers, school board members, and business leaders to stop telling teachers what, when, and how to teach. There may be nothing wrong with telling teachers what kinds of people are needed in the workplace and elsewhere, what kinds of skills and knowledge are needed, but please stop there. Resist the temptation to tell teachers what curriculum to use and how to administer it. To do otherwise is like telling physicians that the same medication and treatment is good for every patient.

One of the greatest incentives for teachers to rise to a new level is to let them know that we have faith they will know what to do to help parents produce a society full of competent, caring, creative people. We need to tell them that we respect their ability to assess the needs of each child and foster his or her optimal growth. If we want to see a revolution in education, just turn teachers loose. Free the slaves and let them unlock their great creative powers!

An article in the March 2002 *Kappan* by Barry McGhan builds a strong case for giving teachers full control over their own reform:

"Only when teachers undertake the responsibility of fixing their own teaching—individually and collectively—will they come to be viewed as professionals, people whose viewpoint will not be discounted by self-styled experts who think they know best how to improve education."

I believe teachers will enthusiastically respond to an invitation to overcome cultural constraints, especially when they are invited to help parents nurture positive human diversity. It will be relatively easy to fashion a system that holds teachers responsible for doing what is possible—in contrast to a system that demands uniformity. One could ask teachers to keep a log of some of the ways they nurture positive differences each week. It could be an agreement between a teacher and parents that each would keep such a log and use it as a point of discussion in periodic assessment meetings. Other ways will be created as we become familiar with a new way of looking at what it means to teach.

One final word about supporting teachers as they nurture positive human diversity: This attitude opens a door of opportunity for us to allow and encourage teachers to be themselves, to be diverse, to fully capitalize on *their own* unique talents and gifts as they interact with children.

Up to now we have asked teachers to function with their own natural abilities hidden. We have expected them to perform according to an imposed cultural pattern as obedient workers on an assembly line with their minds disabled. When we respect teachers as professionals in their efforts to nurture the positive diversity of children we will release a marvelous power for dynamic change in education, both at home and in schools.

While we wait for a new generation of teachers to be prepared, we can give permission to current teachers to use their unique gifts in helping students identify and develop their gifts. It may come as a shock for many teachers to be allowed to create their own lesson plans—as in days of old—but the new freedom will be eagerly embraced by all except those robots who need to be told what to do day by day. They will soon leave the profession and be replaced by people who welcome an intellectual and creative challenge.

༄

Draw Forth
the Latent Potential of Learners

With this principle we give ourselves and teachers permission to care enough to see the good in everyone and draw it out. We give permission to alter the curriculum for each child to discover his or her own gifts and develop them for humanity. We give permission for love to be a vital force in education.

Drawing forth the latent potential of learners is the exact opposite of trying to cram a cleverly crafted body of knowledge into the heads of reluctant learners. It's much easier to respect and support teachers for doing what students are naturally inclined to do than to require them to go against the grain of learning. When students become eager, aggressive participants in their own education, the teachers who draw forth latent potential are elevated to a high level of honor and respect. Teachers serving the needs of students, rather than serving the needs of bureaucrats beholden to powerful corporations, will help us enter a bright new era.

The act of supporting teachers to draw forth and help children develop their unique gifts, talents, and abilities instead of demanding that they standardize students will help usher in the desperately needed revolution in education. When we discover that a child is gifted in math, music, reading, writing, language, art, mechanical skills or whatever, and we nurture the gift, what does this do for student achievement? Although standardized tests are not appropriate, if students were to be given these tests, would the scores increase or decline?

I'm sure it doesn't take the mind of a rocket scientist to see that the overall average scores would skyrocket (excuse the pun). Students would score high in the things they were good at and lower in other areas, but the overall average scores would be much higher. Then, if we take into account the growth that takes place as students are energized from personal asset development to overcome their deficits, we will understand why the average scores would shoot up dramatically. For those who are obsessed with standardized achievement testing, I hasten to point out that these tests are a major contributing factor in the development of a system of education that pressures teachers to force children into a common mold. By eliminating these tests, we can begin to think about creating ways to assess the growth of the latent potential of learners. We can support teachers to draw forth the superb gifts of each special child. Inasmuch as tests drive teaching, we need a new kind of assessment that will call forth a different kind of teaching. I will explain more about this in the next chapter.

ʒ⅌

Respect Autonomy

This principle, like the others, calls for a change in the direction education has been headed during the last 40 or 50 years. During this time, those in control have gradually eroded the right of students to build themselves as well as the right of teachers to use their creative wills to influence learners. The factory model of education, with students viewed as products and teachers viewed as subservient workers, has all but destroyed student autonomy.

If we respect the right of students to build themselves with free will, we must also respect the right of teachers to harness their own wills in their professional callings. To do less than this is to take away a great power, that of creativity—and when creativity is lost, we lose our humanity; we lose a very precious part of ourselves. When we steal autonomy from teachers, students, and parents, we take away volition and the right to shape our own futures. Does this help you to understand the Great Brain Robbery and the reason why we must replace assembly-line education with a totally new system?

ʒ⅌

Invite Inquiry

To respect teachers as professionals as they help students engage in personal inquiry would change the nature of education in schools and in the homes of our culture. Textbooks will no longer be used as the main source of information. Books that have been designed and written to deliver a common body of information into the heads of students will no longer be appropriate.

When we invite student inquiry we will need access to a great variety of sources of information. The school library or information center, accessible to the community for extended hours, will become the center of learning along with inquiry centers, which I described in Chapter Eight. Also, the surrounding community itself, and the web of Internet information will increase in value as places to learn.

What about cost? I've often heard parents and teachers alike complain about the shortage of textbooks for children. When I was an elementary school principal I used to dream of the kind of library we could have if we could have used the money that was wasted on textbooks to spend on exciting, beautiful books, films, recordings, microscopes, binoculars, and other hands on inquiry materials for the library. I figured the cost several times and was amazed at what could have been, if there were to have been a major attitude change on the part of the teachers and the public. Since then, the testing industry has taken another huge bite out of a budget that could better be spent on inquiry materials.

Unfortunately, even today many teachers and parents still do not see the school library as a center for inquiry. I know there are school libraries that remain like the one in a school I was transferred to many years ago. The librarian, Mrs. Bently, was a strict lady who allowed children to enter her sacred sanctum only once a week, class by class, for 30 minutes at a time to check books in and out. If a child had a question at other times, and needed to search for information, s/he had to wait until class library time, usually several days away. The teachers went along with Mrs. Bently's system largely because the tradition of our culture did not support the inquiry method of teaching.

As you can imagine, Mrs. Bently did not fit my vision of how a school librarian should function. After several unsuccessful attempts to get her to change, I was pleased to grant Mrs. Bently her request to transfer to another school and be with her old principal, the one I had replaced. I hired a new librarian, Bonnie Poulson, who opened the library for spontaneous, free-flow inquiry at all times, and we got along just fine. Bonnie was instrumental in making the Great Brain Project as successful as it was, and in helping teachers begin to overcome traditional teaching methods.

Supporting the inquiry method of teaching is much different than supporting teaching that has been shaped by our culture. This is one reason it may be difficult for some people to accept. On the other hand, fears will soon be erased when people see children enthusiastically pursuing information to build their own knowledge.

GOING THE EXTRA MILE ON "THE ROAD LESS TRAVELED BY"

I have a friend in Florida, Marion Brady, who has been trying for many years to convince the education establishment that the performance plateau on which the institution is stuck is attributable primarily to failure to understand and capitalize on the fundamental nature of knowledge, particularly its seamlessly integrated nature.

Marion doesn't discard the traditional subjects and courses, but likens them to random pieces of a jigsaw puzzle handed to learners without the benefit of "a picture on the lid of the puzzle's box." Unable to grasp the whole of which individual school subjects are parts, and integrate them into a single, useful structure of meaning, what is "learned" tends to go into short-term memory, then disappear when exams are over or pressures to perform are removed.

What learners need, he says, is a "master conceptual framework"—a single, easily understood organizer of knowledge that encompasses and integrates everything the learner knows and will ever know.

In fact, he points out, all learners, no matter age or ability, already have and make constant, routine, sophisticated use of such a framework, just are not conscious of doing so. Making sense of reality, they pull from consciousness a particular past, present, or future experience, then (1) locate that experience in space, (2) assign it time dimensions, (3) identify the participating actors, (4) describe the action, (5) assume or attribute cause for the action, and (6) relate the five systemically."

"Analyze any experience," Marion says, "any school subject, any communication, any speculation, any thought, any theory, any dream, and, if it 'makes sense,' the five kinds of information will be the raw material from which it is constructed."

The five, of course, are simply versions of the five familiar, direct questions about a particular reality: Where? When? Who? What? Why? Unfortunately, the questions are so familiar, so mundane-seeming, it is extremely difficult to recognize their pedagogical power. That recognition doesn't ordinarily emerge until learners are first pushed to answer the five questions to an unaccustomed level of comprehensiveness and precision, and then explore their complex, systemic relationships.

The most important task of a general education, he says, is helping learners make their implicitly known organizer explicit—raise it into consciousness so it can be elaborated, refined, and deliberate, formal use made of it to process existing knowledge and generate new knowledge.

I believe that what Marion is advocating is the foundation of all inquiry, and will eventually be taken for granted in all classrooms. For that to happen, however, educators must move past the notion that the task is to teach school subjects rather than make more sense of experience. The most direct means to that end is instruction that helps learners make more sense of the sense-making process.

If teachers will learn to use Brady's system, it will help raise public school teaching to a higher, professional level of respect.

Marion Brady is a retired high school teacher, college professor, district-level administrator, textbook and professional book author, newspaper columnist, and consultant to publishers, states, and foundations. I urge you to contact him and learn of the free on-line course he is offering.

This then is what it means to *support professionalism*. Being sensitive to the needs of individual learners—and meeting those needs—is much different than trying to deliver a set curriculum into the heads of many different kinds of children. It is much more complex, but it is also many times more rewarding. If we work as hard to develop a new system of education as we have to perfect the information delivery system, we will soon see great benefits. Teachers and parents need to shake off the bureaucratic chains and stand up for children. Our very integrity is at stake.

CHAPTER 10

The Sixth Principle: CommUNITY for Great Schools

Never doubt that a small group of thoughtful,
committed citizens can change the world; indeed,
it's the only thing that ever has.

—Margaret Mead

What do Susan Ohanian and Don Perl have in common with the late Rosa Parks? Rosa refused to go to the back of the bus where "blacks" were supposed to sit. Susan and Don are extraordinary teachers who refuse to be slaves to the giant testing industry. All three of these amazing people have a pure, rock-solid integrity.

What if most teachers in America had this kind of integrity? Would they have allowed NCLB to enter their classrooms— or kick it out after they found out what it was? Why do so many teachers meekly submit to doing things they know are harmful to children? I believe teachers did not openly stand up against the No Child Left Behind Law because they did not have a good, alternative reform plan to offer. Now there is a reform plan that most of them do not yet know about—

until they read this book. *Educating for Human Greatness* is a reform plan created by educators (not by business executives and politicians) that invites teachers to harness their integrity and stand for what they intuitively know, deep in their hearts, is good for students.

Who is Susan Ohanian, and why is she one of my heroes? Susan is an extraordinary teacher with unusual intuition of what is good educational practice. She described the classroom as the place she wanted to be, but her missionary zeal provoked her to say "Yes" to a call from Learning Magazine to become staff writer. "I didn't regard it as leaving teaching, which was—and is—my passion in life," she says. "I saw it as an opportunity to extend my reach. The teacher voice wasn't much heard those days and with every column I wrote about my students, about good classroom practice, I felt I was speaking for thousands."

Years later, when Susan became a freelance writer, she had the opportunity to visit classrooms in 26 states. "I saw what good things teachers are doing. My travels made me prouder than ever to call myself "teacher."

Susan's worry that federal/corporate and state policies threaten the very existence of good teaching led her to set up a website in opposition to high stakes testing, No Child Left Behind and then, Race to the Top, which Susan regarded as more dangerous than NCLB. "I coined the word 'Standardisto' in *One Size Fits Few*," says Susan. "Now that term seems so benign. Now we're talking about killers. Make no mistake about it: they are out to destroy public education."

Despite her focus on the corporate agenda to deform schools, Susan also finds space on her websites, www.susanohanian.org and www.StopNationalStandards.org, to celebrate the work of dedicated teachers who have the integrity and strength to resist. She says, "We must never forget to stop and shout 'Hallelujah!' in the presence of good teaching."

Susan has written 24 books. The titles of two show her interest both in the politics of education and in curriculum: *Why Is Corporate America Bashing Our Public Schools?* and *The Great Word Catalogue: FUNdamental Activities for Building Vocabulary.*

I will share part of Don Perl's story in his own words:

"I was faced with the prospect of preparing my eighth grade students for high stakes standardized testing in the fall of 2000 - the test to be administered in February of 2001. The more I studied this concept of high stakes testing, the more abhorrent it became to me, and the more I saw it as a violation of my egalitarian principles as an educator.

I was teaching in an inner city junior high school in Greeley, Colorado, which in 2000 - 2001 had been converted into a middle school. About half of my students spoke Spanish as their first language, and since English wasn't their home language, they were at a disadvantage in this testing regimen.

I was also one of only a few bilingual teachers at our school and was often called to translate conversations between administrators and parents. I saw parents, wanting the best for their children, struggling to understand a foreign system. I remembered the phrase "in loco parentis" that I had heard often as an aspiring teacher. We don't want any harm to come to our children. This testing mania was harmful to them - it pitted them against each other. Thus, after much deliberation, reflection, and study, I decided that I could not in good conscience administer the test. And so I committed an act of civil disobedience by refusing to administer the Colorado Student Assessment (CSAP) tests.

In January of 2001, in fact on the day we honor the memory of Dr. Martin Luther King Jr. I composed and sent letters to policy makers, legislators, the local and state school board and the governor's office. Here is what I said:

The more I have researched the issue of high stakes standardized testing, the more I have come to the realization that these tests are antithetical to 1) the egalitarian premise of public schools and 2) undermine the dignity of the teaching profession.

Regarding issue number 1 - Generally students who fare well are those who have a literary background, and are from Western European professional or middle class families. Thus, the tests further polarize our already polarized community. Minority students, students whose language is other than English, are disadvantaged from the moment they bubble in their names.

Regarding the second issue - the undermining of the teaching profession - there seems to be an underlying concept that all teachers need is a manual to follow and all will go well in the classroom. They don't realize that the makeup of every class is different. Teaching is an art, a science, and a calling, all of which defy a lock-step manual. No test can measure citizenship, co-operation, and compassion. The professional in the classroom strives to develop thoughtful and meaningful assessments which connect curricula with individual learning styles. For us to subject children to one dimensional high stakes testing is nothing short of educational malpractice. Therefore, I must respectfully decline to administer the test."

Don was suspended for two weeks without pay for refusing to administer the tests. He goes on to say:

"When I returned to my teaching assignment, the atmosphere at school was so negatively charged that I decided to make that year my last. I landed a teaching position at our local university in the department of Hispanic Studies, and my new colleagues encouraged me to keep speaking out against the injustices of standardized testing."

Don Perl did continue to speak out. He now heads the Colorado Coalition for Better Education and now speaks out very convincingly through his web site–www.thecbe.org.

What are the lessons we can learn from Rosa Parks, Susan Ohanian and Don Perl? Integrity stands at the top of the list. It includes *intuition* to know in one's heart what is good for children and the *courage* to be true to oneself against all odds. What Shakespeare said, as he gave voice to Polonius in Hamlet, is worth repeating in this context:

> *This above all: to thine own self be true,*
> *And it must follow as the night the day*
> *Thou canst not be false to any man.*

Being true to yourself means that you may want to do some of the following things:

- Refuse to do anything that you feel in your heart is harmful to children. Convince administrators by showing them a better way.
- Let students decide if they want to take standardized tests. They can submit a request in writing to be exempted.
- If you are a teacher, let parents know that they have a right to request an exemption for their child.
- If you are a parent, request to the school in writing that your child be exempted from taking the standardized testing.
- If you are a teacher, explain why you refuse to administer standardized achievement testing.
- Refuse to cheat kindergarten and first grade students of learning from curious inquiry. Respect their differences and timetable for reading and math. Do not abuse them with commercial reading and math programs. Provide ample time for art, science, play and social interaction.
- Diligently strive to raise your teaching to a higher level as implied by the concepts of *Educating for Human Greatness*

⅋

RECAPITULATION
of Educating FOR Greatness

Much water has gone under the education bridge since the first edition of this book was published some years ago. The U.S. Department of Education relentlessly continues its ill-conceived push for student uniformity. Now, as I write these words, a huge mistake is about to be made under the banner, "National Standards." The National Governors Association Center for Best Practices (NGA Center) and the Council of Chief State School Officers (CCSSO) are unveiling a plan to develop common English-language Arts and Mathematics standards across the nation. They call it the "Common Core State Standards Initiative." Subject matter specialists have decided what all students should know and be able to do at each grade level. Achievement tests will be administered to track and compare progress in building student uniformity across the states.

"High Standards" is a concept that is just as limiting as was "No Child Left Behind." You will be labeled unpatriotic if you are against it. Now I ask, "High standards for what? For student uniformity?" Why not have high standards for nurturing positive human diversity? Believe it or not, we can have a school system that helps each child excel in what they were born to be good at. Those who were born with a gift to be outstanding in math, can become so. Those gifted in music can excel in music. Those in art, likewise. Pick any skill or subject matter discipline and there will be some who are destined to make a valuable contribution to society in that discipline. But if you try to make students alike in everything, you will rarely find one who will excel in anything.

Small groups of thoughtful, UNITED citizens will begin

to change the education world when they convincingly show a better purpose for public and private education. Many people have their minds set on a false purpose—*student achievement in curriculum*. This purpose has effectively stopped all efforts of authentic reform. Remember George Odiorne? I will paraphrase his words: "*Most people are caught in the curriculum trap. They are so obsessed with curriculum, they lose sight of what it is for and student achievement in curriculum becomes a false goal, an end in and of itself.*" This false goal for education keeps people trying harder and harder to do something that is not only impossible, but harmful—making students all alike and equal in knowledge and skills.

There is a way to break out of our mental jail. We can simplify and make clear the real purpose of education so parents and teachers can unite as partners. I've already related how we surveyed thousands of parents in six school communities to determine their needs for children— and we were surprised to learn that student achievement in subject matter content was not the top priority.

I believe we discovered some universal truths that put students, parents, teachers, and subject matter content in a correct relationship. These truths make possible an alliance that is not possible when the school system is trying to standardize students. An enormous change will occur when we adopt a purpose that explains what schools are really for—a purpose that parents and teachers can unite around—this one, for example:

Help each student develop the qualities of greatness and become a valuable contributor to society.

ૐ

THE POWER OF UNITY

With human greatness as the main purpose of education we can free ourselves from thinking of student achievement in subject matter content as the main goal of education. There is great power that comes from this different perspective. Students, teachers, and parents can now join hands as full partners to grow greatness in one another. If we want children to become contributors, we must harness curriculum to help them grow—in the characteristics most likely to result in contributive behavior—the dimensions of human greatness. Since the first edition of this book was published, a group of "thoughtful, committed citizens" organized the Educating for Human Greatness Alliance and added four more dimensions to the original three: **Initiative, Imagination, Intuition** and **Integrity.**

Now we have seven dimensions of greatness that form a comprehensive framework for redesigning education in each community. These dimensions add up to a strong, courageous character in each amazing child.

ૐ

CURRICULUM AS SERVANT

This is the new vision that we propose for education: Aim for goals that can be kept constantly in mind and make subject matter content work for us. It's in stark contrast to the present system wherein people are in subjection to obsolete subject matter content, textbook publishers, the testing industry, corporate executives and uninformed politicians. With **Identity, Interaction, Inquiry, Initiative, Imagination, Intuition** and **Integrity** as new goals, curriculum becomes our servant (instead of boss)—it changes everything! If parents and teachers want to develop contributors, they will unite to fulfill seven deep yearnings of children:

- The yearning to be a respected individual with unique talents. (Identity)
- The need for healthy relationships with others. (Interaction)
- The need to learn – to satisfy and magnify curiosity. (Inquiry)
- Autonomy – the need to exercise agency and be in control of oneself. (Initiative)
- The need to be creative, innovative and solve problems. (Imagination)
- The sixth sense – the need to feel truth and learn with one's heart. (Intuition)
- The need to be an honest, upright, contributing citizen. (Integrity)

Thinking of curriculum as a *means* of accomplishing higher goals—the seven dimensions of greatness—is a revolutionary way of thinking about education. Without this kind of purpose, student achievement in subject matter content is meaningless. Curriculum becomes a relentless taskmaster. It's the whip used by bureaucrats to control what teachers and students do, but prevents them from responding to the needs of individual students.

Some habits are very hard to break, especially those that are habits of culture. To go against the dominant culture of a country is particularly difficult. Count Leo Tolstoy said it best:

"I know that most (men and women), including those at ease with problems of the greatest complexity, can seldom accept even the simplest and most obvious truth if it be such as would oblige them to admit the falsity of conclusions which they have delighted in explaining to colleagues, which they have proudly taught to others, and which they have woven, thread by thread into the fabric of their lives. "

In this book I have tried to explain how a different mental focus changes the way we use curriculum, or subject matter content, in schools and homes. By now you probably sense the sweeping changes implied by such a view. Even if you can break your own mental habits, powerful political forces will assuredly arise to try to thwart any attempts to change public education in any significant way. Each alliance of thoughtful citizens, who are committed to Educating for Human Greatness, must be prepared for attacks by special interest groups, including some local boards of education and even educators who bought into No Child Left Behind or National Standards and invested much time and money to help perfect the conveyor belt system. *Educating for Human Greatness* is a powerful concept that can break down the walls of resistance.

Why do we need a better main goal and purpose for education than student achievement in subject matter content?

Every single year for the last 30 years (at least) the Bureau of Justice Statistics has recorded an increase in America's prison population, reporting over 2,300,000 incarcerated citizens in state and federal prisons in 2008. In 2007 the PEW Research Center reported that the USA incarcerates more people per capita than any other country for a cost of nearly $50 billion per year! Over 80% of the prison space in this country has been built in the last 20 years! And they are filled with a very high percentage of dropouts.

I know about this first hand. During the time when our school was formulating its main purpose of education, Davis County was in the process of building a new, larger jail and court complex. Soon after it was completed, the county commissioners announced a need to add a $25 million 400-bed addition to the new jail, which caused the largest tax increase ever. This fueled our conviction that it is much better, and less expensive, to spend taxpayer money on schools to develop great human beings who are contributors (not burdens) to society than it is to incarcerate/rehabilitate them.

In his book, *Shadow Children ~ Understanding Education's #1 Issue*, Dr. Anthony Dallmann-Jones states: "During NCLB and all this focus on testing to standards, the number of dropouts increased and the prison population right along with it! Those business people interested in education can perhaps better grasp this kind of talk: **It costs almost $64,000 per year to incarcerate youth. It costs an average of $8500 a year if they are in school.** This should make even the most educationally ignorant members of the business and political communities begin to see less value in common standards and more value in liberating schools from them. Instead, we need schools that are more relevant, meaningful, exciting and inviting to our youth. We need to start NOW."

The problem is serious and growing. Many of those who are alienated from standardized education often become burdens on society. Elaine Jarvik, in a newspaper article, "The Rise of Rudeness," tells about an epidemic of rude behavior exhibited by many high school students. She writes that "teachers complain that the number of students who are openly rude is on the rise and that, in administrators meetings, the principals are constantly talking about the deterioration of respect." Bullying is one form of this rudeness that is rapidly increasing as are dropouts, who often turn to drugs, and crime. There is much evidence that public schools, for one reason or another, do not meet the needs of a good many students. How many classes have students, in Jr. and Senior High schools, who do not want to be there? Just ask teachers. They will tell you, "If it were not for the class disturbers, we could really accomplish something." One answer to this problem is to guide students into courses they see a need to take rather than requiring them to take classes that don't fit their perceived needs.

What is the difference between schools that aim for student accomplishment in a required core curriculum and those that aim to help students become contributors to the family, school and community?

The first big difference is parent involvement. When parents and teachers unite to help students grow in the seven dimensions of human greatness, amazing things begin to happen. This kind of relationship is not possible when student achievement in curriculum is the main goal. Can you imagine what happens in a home when parents join the school effort to magnify a child's curiosity, for example—or help the school identify and develop a child's individual talents—and build his or her determination to be a contributor?

The second difference involves the choice between student uniformity or student individuality. Those involved in Educating for Greatness hold student Identity as a major priority and do not try to make students alike in knowledge or skills, but help them develop their unique talents and gifts—and use their abilities to contribute to the school, family and community. Individual differences in background of experiences, learning styles and timetable for learning are respected.

The third major difference has to do with the role of curriculum. In conventional education, student achievement in a state-sanctioned core curriculum is the main goal and purpose for education. It is what is tested and assessed. In educating for greatness, curriculum is a *tool* to help students grow as contributors to society—to grow in the dimensions of greatness that make contributing possible. Thousands of topics are available for students to use in developing individual greatness. Students are assessed in their growth in Identity, Interaction, Inquiry, Initiative, Imagination, Intuition and Integrity. (See "A Tool for Assessing School Effectiveness in Helping Students Grow as Contributors to Society." P.16)

A fourth major difference is student learning and achievement. Learning, that is the result of students searching for answers to their own questions, is deeper and more enduring than learning that is imposed or required. Students engage in self-chosen home *study,* not home *work. Every Child Can Excel* in something, if s/he is given enough choices. This is what it means to make curriculum fit, and respond to the needs of each unique student. Finally, I can't emphasize this difference enough – **Students learn reading, writing, and math skills better when they are taught as tools of inquiry, interaction and identity than when they are taught as ends in and of themselves.**

ꝛ⚹

The Ultimate Difference—Professional Teaching Versus Conventional Teaching

Is there a difference in how teachers perform, a difference in how they practice their craft? William Arthur Ward described some differences thusly: "The mediocre teacher tells. The good teacher explains. The superior teacher demonstrates. The great teacher inspires."

In chapter 9, I reported on a study conducted by researchers who studied video tapes to learn why Japanese students excel in mathematics high above students in the U.S.. Stigler and Hiebert reported that teachers in three countries teach the way they were taught in their culture. In the United States the teaching style was mostly telling, explaining and demonstrating followed by student practice. In Japan, teachers invited students to discuss and analyze various ways to solve a problem to arrive at an answer. Now, Stigler and Hiebert report, in an extension of their 1995 study, that, in spite of much effort during recent years to improve mathematics teaching, nearly all mathematics teachers in the United States are still teaching the way they were taught in schools they attended.

They are still using direct instruction—telling, explaining and demonstrating.

What is the message of this? What does "teaching that inspires" look like? Plutarch said many years ago, "*The mind is not a vessel to be filled, but a fire to be kindled.*" If this is true, why do so many mathematics teachers in our country teach by telling, explaining and demonstrating to fill student's minds? What does it mean to kindle the fire? How do we kindle the fire of curiosity that every person is born with?

With curriculum as a servant, rather than boss over students, teachers hold students responsible for their own learning, growth and development. This changes their roles. Students are no longer passive absorbers of a fixed and static curriculum presented to them with unsolicited, direct instruction, but are expected to magnify their curiosity and aggressively seek knowledge through inquiry and develop their own talents, gifts, interests and abilities. Teachers spend much of their time creating opportunities and help for students to exercise curiosity and develop personal and group quests.

In the Educating for Greatness model, teachers try to replace relatively easy *direct instruction,* (telling, explaining and demonstrating) which usually results in shallow, temporary knowledge, with a much more sophisticated interaction with students and parents. They engage in the fine art of *drawing forth* from each student the latent potential—the questions, powers, gifts, knowledge and abilities that lie within each amazing child. Classes become inquiry-centered because teachers know that "*knowledge acquired under compulsion obtains no hold on the mind.*"(Plato) Professional teaching is in stark contrast to "direct instruction" that requires home "work" rather than self-chosen home *study.* **The power to draw forth the latent potential of each child through love, skillful questioning and listening raises teaching to a higher, more professional level.**

The Framework for Redesigning Education in Your CommUNITY

Each of the seven dimensions offers a doorway into a better approach that promises better results—more growth in knowledge and skills—than education for student uniformity. You are invited to use the space under each dimension to list your own strategies for accomplishing it in your home or school. We have suggested some which worked for us that you might consider trying.

1. IDENTITY – A strong, positive sense of self-worth based on the development of individual talents, gifts, interests and abilities. Confidence, competence and a strong desire to be a contributor to home, school and community. Answers the question, Who am I and what can I become?

   ### LIST POSSIBLE STRATEGIES
   ### for NUTURING IDENTITY:

   1. The "Shining Stars" Talent Development Program. (See Appendix C.)

   2. _____

   3. _____

2. INQUIRY – A curious attitude. The ability to ask penetrating questions and pursue a quest for answers and for better questions. Reading and math are taught as processes of inquiry. Answers the question, "How can I learn?"

POSSIBLE STRATEGIES:

1. The Great Brain Project. (See Appendices D & E.)

2. Provide a variety of interesting reading material and time for silent sustained, voluntary reading.

3. Parents and teachers show many examples of curious inquiry.

4. Give frequent math experiences in observing, counting, weighing, measuring, comparing and solving real problems.

5. Interview authorities—people who know things about various subjects.

6. Use the 22 question-starter words.

7. _____

8. _____

3. INTERACTION – Respect for others. Courtesy, kindness, caring, communication and cooperation. What kind of relationships shall I develop with other people?

STRATEGIES:

1. Organize a school post office for in-school communication.

2. Parents and teachers set an example of love and kind interaction.

3. Express appreciation often.

4. _____

5. _____

4. INITIATIVE – Self-directed learning, autonomy, confidence and will power. How can I use my agency to control my learning and behavior?

STRATEGIES:

1. Provide time for students to plan, organize and pursue their own learning.

2. _____

3. _____

5. IMAGINATION – The ability of the mind to be creative and resourceful. In how many ways can I use my mind to invent new ideas and better ways of doing things?

STRATEGIES:

1. Provide experiences for students to express themselves with many kinds of art materials.

2. _____

3. _____

4. _____

5. _____

6. INTUITION – Insight. (Immediate apprehension of the mind without reasoning.) Emotional intelligence. The sixth sense. Recognizing truth with the heart. Humility. How can I develop my heart to feel the difference between truth and falsity?

STRATEGIES:

1. Provide for examination and discussions of various forms of advertising.

2. Often provide experiences for students to listen to great music, see and produce great art, hear stories and poetry that touches their hearts.

3. Provide many opportunities for students to experience nature with all of their senses and creatively respond.

4. _____

5. _____

7. INTEGRITY – Moral uprightness, honesty, wholeness, and strength of character. What can I do to be true to myself and others at all times?

STRATEGIES:

1. Provide frequent discussions and frequent practice in predicting the results and consequences of various choices and decisions.

2. _____

꙲

Evaluation, Assessment and Accountability

The right kind of evaluation is a critical element in changing a school from one bent on meeting the needs of politicians and business leaders to one that is tenaciously trying to meet the needs of children. If we really want to improve the quality of what teachers do, we will hold them responsible for working with parents to meet the needs of individual children rather than futilely striving to standardize students.

Who assesses the quality of a child's work in a class s/he has chosen? For deep learning to occur, a wise teacher will help children evaluate the quality of their own work and learn from mistakes. This can happen if parents and teachers use subject matter content as a tool to help students grow in the dimensions of greatness. On the other hand, if curriculum is our boss—if student achievement in content is our main goal, it forces teachers to try to shape students to fit a common mold, an impossible assignment.

If evaluation instruments call for student growth in greatness—if curriculum is our servant—it makes teachers accountable for doing that which is possible, but rather difficult—meeting the needs of individual children. The evaluation instruments in Appendix B, one for young children and one for older, were used by the courageous teachers and parents united as partners in two schools to begin changing their small part of the world.

Parents, teachers, and students all mark these "report cards," inasmuch as all are responsible, and use them in assessment meetings. You can use these as a pattern to develop your own assessment tools and begin the process of making a mighty change in your heart and in our system of public education. The main thing to remember is to evaluate what we are trying to accomplish—growth in student greatness. Because assessment drives teaching, we need to change to a form of assessment that calls forth great, inspired teaching, teaching that nurtures positive differences and draws forth the latent potential of every precious person. You can also use the "Tool for Assessing School Effectiveness in Helping Students Grow as Contributors to Society" that was presented in Chapter One.

In our new system of education FOR greatness there is an important concept that must be kept in mind: Evaluation is an important part of the learning process. This means that students should be helped to assess the quality of their own work and make revisions accordingly. External, authoritarian evaluation is useful only to the extent that it facilitates student self-assessment. Parents and teachers can ask questions that result in student introspection and self-awareness. The worst kind of evaluation is that which separates the student from his work and then is stamped with only a letter grade.

❧

The Sleeping Giant – A Higher Vision

A different concept, education for human greatness, is sorely needed, not only in the United States, but also all over the world. There are unique gifts, talents, and abilities lying dormant in millions of children and adults waiting to be awakened and developed for the benefit of humankind. There are many artists on the order of Rembrandt, writers on the level of Shakespeare, scientists equal to Einstein, musicians like Mozart, Bach, and Beethoven, and humanitarians like Mother Teresa—millions of people with latent gifts waiting for the special love that you and others like you can use to draw them out. Every one of us has special qualities of greatness that we can begin to develop and use immediately.

In this book I have tried to build a case for refocusing education. I have tried to show that nurturing positive human diversity is immensely better than trying to do the impossible task of standardizing students. With six pivotal principles and seven dimensions of human greatness, I have set forth a vision of education that sees latent, potential greatness in everyone. It is a vision that invites parents, teachers, and children to get acquainted with their own wonderful selves and use their unique gifts and talents to benefit the world. I believe this focus is urgently needed to rescue our public schools from the tight grasp of the U.S. Department of Education and State Departments that are trying to standardize students. You are invited to take the lead in introducing this focus to the people of your community. When enough people become united we will change the world.

⋇

Intuition, Integrity and Courage

I started this chapter by telling about two amazing people who are walking their talk—Susan Ohanian and Don Perl. Now you have a choice. You can follow their examples of intuition, integrity and courage or you can continue to be swept along by false traditions. You can use this book as a manual or handbook for creative collaboration to build a school system in your community that nurtures individual potential. Schools can become places where parents, teachers and students all learn how to help one another grow in greatness.

We invite you to share your ideas and experiences. Perhaps, one day, we can convince the U.S. Department of Education to change its unconstitutional role from being a dictator of educational policies to that of a resource repository of ideas and strategies for accomplishing this main purpose for public education:

Appendix A

Parent Priorities

Priorities for the education of _____(student)
for the_____school year

Please rate the following educational goals 1 through 10, according to your child's needs in terms of what you feel is most to least important for the school to help you accomplish:

___ **Health and Physical Development**
Nutrition habits; physical fitness; strength, endurance, agility, and skill in sports, games, and life activities.

___ **Human Relations and Communication**
Getting along with others, leadership, cooperation, courtesy, respect, listening, speaking, reading, and writing.

___ **Identity and Individuality**
Self-esteem, self-confidence, self-discipline, responsibility, moral character, and the development of individual talents, gifts, interests, and abilities.

___ **Inquiry, Thinking, Learning**
Curiosity, eagerness to learn, study skills and habits, problem solving, creativity, and decision making.

___ **Science and Math**
Knowledge and skill in mathematics and the physical sciences.

___ **Arts**
Knowledge, skill, and appreciation for literature, music, dance, and the visual and performing arts.

___ **Work**
Initiative, self-motivation, self-direction, persistence, following through, and evaluating work; understanding of attitudes, knowledge, and abilities needed for various vocations.

___ **Responsible Citizenship**
Respect for and understanding of the workings of a democracy, appreciation for political processes and free enterprise.

___ **Environment**
Respect and maintenance of personal and public property, enjoying and protecting nature.

___ **Other** (describe):

_____
_____
_____
_____

Appendix B

An Assessment of Student Growth in the
Three Dimensions of Human Greatness

Date _____

Evaluation for _____

Please indicate how much you feel this child is growing in each of the categories listed below:

Identity	Comments:
1. Self-esteem, self-respect, and self-confidence	
2. Sense of responsibility for his/her own learning and behavior	
3. Awareness and development of his/her unique strengths, talents, gifts, interest, and abilities	
Interaction	
4. Kindness, trust, thoughtfulness, tolerance, and respect for others	
5. Social attitudes and skills -- the ability to listen with understanding, express ideas, and get along with others	
6. Enjoyment and ability to express him/herself in writing	
7. Responsible citizenship, understanding of the workings of the democratic process, respect for environment and laws	
Inquiry	
8. Enjoyment of Learning	
9. Enjoyment of School	
10. Curiosity, initiative, self-direction, and independence in trying to learn.	
11. Studying and seeking information from a variety of sources	
12. Ability and desire to read for recreation and personal growth	
13. Ability and desire to use knowledge to create, invent, think, and solve problems	

Signature of evaluator _____

Appendix B, Part 2

Student Self-Assessment (Early Grades)

Directions: The parent or teacher is to read each question orally to the student, who then draws a smiling face, a frowning face, or an "in-between face" to represent his/her feelings about the question.

Identity: ☹ ☺ 😐	Example Answers
1. Do you do a good job of learning?	☺😐☹
2 Are you good at some things?	😐
3. Does your teacher like you?	☺
4. Do your classmates like you?	☺
Inquiry:	
1. Do you learn the things you want to learn?	😐
2. Do you ask a lot of questions in your class?	☹
3. Do you read outside of school?	☺
4. Do you like to figure things out by yourself?	☺
Interaction:	
1. Do you get along with other students?	☹
2. How do you behave in school?	😐
3. Do other people listen to your ideas?	☺
4. Do you get along with your family?	☺
5. Do you like to write?	☹

Name_____ Date _____

Appendix C

SHINING STARS POSSIBILITIES

ART
painting, oil, water, acrylics
drawing
whittling
carving
sculpting
making ceramics
making puppets
kite-making
paper sculpting
wood constructions
papier-mâché
photography
movie making
video production

WRITING
stories
plays
poems
essays
shadow plays
skits

CRAFTS
cross-stitch
sewing
knitting
crochet
embroidery
quilting
tatting
weaving
textile paintings
cooking
model building
handyman
mechanics

DRAMATICS
giving humorous readings
telling stories
debating
acting
giving speeches
reciting poetry
being an emcee
performing skits
performing magic tricks

DANCING
ballet
tap
clogging
creative
mime

MISC.
detective
finger math, Chisenbop
pet training
equestrian
checkers, chess

MUSICAL
singing solo
singing duet
quartet, barbershop
instrument playing
homemade instruments
band

PHYSICAL
aerobics
juggling
sprinting
distance running
tightrope walking
high jumping
wrestling
weight training
playing basketball
arm wrestling
Frisbee throwing
basketball shooting, dribbling
long jumping
rope jumping
dart throwing
cheerleading
trick bicycle riding
marble shooting
baton drill
archery
gymnastics
balance
running

HOBBIES
_____
_____
_____
_____

This list is not intended to be final. Please feel free to add any that might have been overlooked.

Appendix D
Great Brain Signup Sheet

THE GREAT BRAIN PROJECT
—OFFICIAL ENTRY BLANK—

On this_____ day of_____,20____,I,_____do
hereby enroll in the Great Brain Project of _____School. With
my parents' help I have chosen the subject_____to study
in great depth until I feel qualified and prepared to give a presentation to my friends,
relatives, and classmates.

I AGREE TO:

1. Prepare a list of stimulating questions with which to guide my research.

2. Study diligently at school, at home, and in the community.

3. Keep a record of my findings and plan an interesting, creative way to share my new knowledge with others.

4. Let my teacher know when I am ready to make a Great Brain presentation.

I understand that diligent participation in this project may qualify me for a Great Brain award on one of four levels:

It will also entitle me to membership in the Great Brain Club.

I/We the parent(s) of _____
do agree to become partners with my/our child and the school to assist him/her in the chosen quest.

Student's Signature _____

Parent's Signature _____

Appendix E

Great Brain Evaluation

For _____

	Points	Specialist 1	Expert 2	Mastermind 4	Genius 8
Gathering Knowledge					
1. **Questions**					
Quantity					
Quality					
2. **Recording Information**					
Quantity					
Quality					
3. **Reading**					
(Bibliography)					
4. **Other Resources**					
(Interviews, Museums, etc.)					
5. **Creative Product(s) of Original Thinking**					
Presentation					
6. **Loud and Clear**					
7. **Own Words**					
8. **Expression**					
9. **Enthusiasm**					
10. **Holds Audience**					
11. **Visuals**					
12. **Effort**					
13. **Fielding Questions**					
Total Points					

Specialist	10 – 20 points
Expert	21 – 50 points
Mastermind	51 – 100 points
Genius	101 – 120 points

THE SIX PRINCIPLES OF EDUCATING FOR HUMAN GREATNESS

VALUE POSITIVE HUMAN DIVERSITY
Cherish every person as a unique individual.

DRAW FORTH POTENTIAL
Help learners discover and develop their latent talents.

RESPECT AUTONOMY
Restore freedom and responsibility to every learner.

INVITE INQUIRY
Help students develop an insatiable curiosity
and hunger for knowledge.

SUPPORT PROFESSIONALISM
Encourage teachers who live by these principles.

UNITE FOR GREATNESS
Parents and teachers join to help children grow
in human greatness.

The Original Educating for Human Greatness Alliance Members

Deserving much of the credit for refining the EfHG concept:

Lawrence Baines – Judith Daso Herb Chair in Adolescent Literacy at the University of Toledo. lbaines@UTNet.UToledo.edu

Dr. Laurence A Becker - Served 10 years as English Department Chair at St. Stephen's Episcopal School and has worked with autistic savant artists since 1976. He produced the award-winning documentary film "With Eyes Wide Open", and is currently writing a monthly essay for *Autism Today* RBecker64@aol.com

Emmanuel Bernstein – Veteran public school educator of all ages, an educational researcher, and a school guidance counselor. He wrote the book, *The Secret Revolution: A Psychologist's Adventures in Education.* mannyber@yahoo.com

Kenneth Bernstein - National Board Certified Teacher in Maryland. Now in his 14th year of teaching, he came to education after a long career in data processing in both the public and private sectors. He has served as a resource and advisor on educational matters to a number of candidates for and members of the U. S. House and Senate. kber@earthlink.net or teacherken@gmail.com

Renate N. Caine, Researcher, psychologist, author. Director, Natural Learning Research Institute .www.cainelearning.com

Doug Christensen, Emeritus State Commissioner of Public Education for Nebraska, author, and professor. dougchrisensen111@gmail.com

Dr. Boyd R. Cox – Educator with 25 years experience as an elementary teacher, 1 ½ years as the director of the Utah Boys Ranch school, and taught basic mathematics and electronics for 8 years at community college. coxbo@msn.com

Dr. Don Glines, Ph.D. – Director of the Educational Futures Projects in Sacramento, CA and at his Wilson School in Minnesota, acclaimed as an innovative, cradle-to-grave learning center, he has focused on personalized learning and educational alternatives for everyone. (916) 392-1946

Alfie Kohn - Author of eleven books. He has been described by *Time* magazine as "perhaps the country's most outspoken critic of education's fixation on grades [and] test scores." www.alfiekohn.org

Philip Kovacs - Former high school English teacher now teaching teachers at the University of Alabama in Huntsville. He organized the Educator Roundtable on the internet and has worked toward dismantling NCLB. philipkovacs@yahoo.com

Stephen Krashen - Developed the first comprehensive theory of second language acquisition and is the co-inventor of the Natural Approach. His current books are *Summer Reading: Program and Evidence, English Learners in American Classrooms*, and *English Fever*. skrashen@yahoo.com

Michael Mendizza - Author, educator, documentary filmmaker and founder of Touch the Future, a nonprofit learning design center. He co-authored *Magical Parent-Magical Child* with Joseph Chilton Pearce. www.ttfuture.org www.nurturing.us michael@ttfuture.org

Dr. MaryBeth Merritt - Educator, scientist, parent, artist and activist championing holistic education for close to 20 years. And is a founder of Four Winds (www.fourwindsgreatbarrington.org), a non-profit educational organization.

Dr. Deborah Meier, Educator for 40 plus years. Author of *In the Power of Their Ideas* and other books. deborah.meier@gmail.com

Dr. Ronald J. Newell, Ed.D. - Director of Evaluation and Assessment for EdVisions Schools, was a founder of the Minnesota New Country School and EdVisions Cooperative, and has published three books on the subject. He was formerly a high school history teacher, mentor teacher, and college professor.

Nel Noddings – Lee L. Jacks Professor of Childhood Education, Emerita at Stanford University. Her latest book is *When School Reform Goes Wrong.* noddings@stanford.edu

Christopher Nye - Retired professor and college administrator, vice president of The Myrin Institute (an operating foundation), children's book author (*The Old Shepherd's Tale*, 2004, 2008*)*, and poet (*Poems Out of Thin Air*, 2008). He now co-leads an education initiative at The Orion Society to build a constituency for spirited, whole-child education. cnye@orionsociety.org

Susan Ohanian – Longtime teacher and prolific writer on education issues. She maintains a website in opposition to the corporate-politico takeover of schools and the standardization of curriculum. susano@gmavt.net

Mary Orlando - Has been a Montessori educator for the past 40 years. She is currently assistant principal at Villa Montessori Charter School in Phoenix, AZ. morlando@villamontessori.com

Don Perl – Educator of 35 years, who has taught in the public schools of Colorado for 20 years, is a high-stakes test resister and is presently an adjunct professor of Spanish at the University of Northern Colorado. dperl@myexcel.com

Lu Pilgrim – An advocate of project and place-based learning with 50 years experience as a public and independent school teacher and administrator, is on the faculty at Pacific Oaks College. pilgrims@mcn.org

Phoebe Plank – Teacher for 15 years, who is currently volunteering in an alternative school to bring opportunities for Educating for Human Greatness to students, teachers and administrators. plankphoebe@yahoo.com

David Polochanin - Teaches Language Arts in Glastonbury, CT., and has published articles on education and other subjects, appearing in *Education Week* and *Middle Ground.* He has written for the *Providence Journal*, the *Boston Globe, Christian Science Monitor*, and *Hartford Courant.* polochanind@glastonburyus.org

Faith Denise Rossell – Teacher, Florida, fdrosse@gmail.com

Dorothy Rupert - Retired Senator and State Representative from Boulder, Colorado (1986-2001). Rupert was a high school English teacher and counselor for Boulder and Fairview High Schools (Boulder, CO) for 35 years. She teaches courses at The University of Colorado (Boulder campus). In 2005, Dorothy Rupert was nominated for the Nobel Peace Prize. dorothyrupert@earthlink.net

Dr. Yvonne Siu-Runyan – Former public school teacher and professor emerita at the University of Northern Colorado and a current member of the presidential team for the National Council Teachers of English. She has 40 years of professional educational experiences. hanalei@indra.com

William Spady – Author of five books, and a key developer of the "HeartLight" model of learning and living described in Neale Donald Walsch's *Conversations With God* books. He is the current Director of the New Possibilities Network and taught at Harvard University and OISE early in his career.billspady@earthlink.net

Darrell Stoddard – Founder of the Pain Research Institute www.healpain.net and author of *Pain Free for Life*. stoddard@healpain.net

Cooper Zale – Parent of two children, who unschooled through their high school years, and is blogging at www.leftyparent.com and can be reached at czale@socal.rr.com

Bibliography & Suggested Reading

Allen, J. (1902). *As a Man Thinketh*. Mt. Vernon, NY: Peter Pauper Press.

Armstrong, T. (1991). Awakening Your Child's Natural Genius: Enhancing Curiosity, Creativity, and Learning Ability. Los Angeles, Jeremy P. Tarcher, Inc.

Ballam, M. (2001). *The Creativity Factor, 2CDs* Logan, Utah. Phoenix Productions, Canterbury Lane, 84321.

Caine, R. (2010). Making Connections: Natural Learning, Technology and the Human Brain. Columbia MO: Teachers College Press.

Caine, R. N., Caine, G. and McClintic, C. and Klimek, K. (2009). 12 Brain/Mind *Learning Principles* in Action: Developing *Executive Functions of the Human Brain* (2nd. Edition). Thousand Oaks, CA: Corwin Press.

Character Education Network, National Center for Youth Issues. TN: Chattanooga.

Combs, A. W. (1979). *Myths in Education—Beliefs that Hinder Progress and their Alternatives*. Boston: Allyn and Bacon.

Dallmann-Jones, A. (2010). *Shadow Children: Understanding Education's #1 Issue*. Lancaster, PA: RLD Publications.

Darling-Hammond, L. (2010) *The Flat World and Education: How America's Commitment to Equity Will Determine Our Future*. New York, NY: Teachers College Press.

Davis, J., (2009). *Parental influence, school readiness and early academic achievement of African American boys*. The Journal of Negro Education. July.

Eisner, E. (1985). *Beyond Creating, The place for art in America's schools*. Getty Center for Education in the Arts. p. 69.

Elkind, D. (2001). *The Hurried Child*. Reading, MA: Addison-Wesley.

Engel, A. (2009). *Seeds of tomorrow: Solutions for Improving our Children's Education.* Boulder CO: Paradigm Publishers.

Gardner, H. (1985). *The Frames of Mind: Theory of Multiple Intelligences.* New York: Basic Books.

Gardner, H. (2000). *Intelligence Reframed: Multiple Intelligences for the 21ˢᵗ Century.* New York: Basic Books.

Gibbons, M. (1974). Walkabout: *Searching for the right passage from childhood and school.* Phi Delta Kappan: May.

Greenberg, D. (1991). *Free at last: The Sudbury Valley School.*

Framingham, MA: Sudbury Valley School Press.

Guilford, J. P. (1968). Intellectual factors in productive thinking. In *Productive thinking in education.* Washington, D.C.: National Education Association.

Hanks, M. D. (1977). *The Gift of Self.* Salt Lake City: Bookcraft.

Hansel, L., Skinner, B. and Rothberg, I. C.. (2001). *The Changing Teaching Environment.* Washington: Institute for Education Policy Studies.

Huerta, G. (2009). *Educational Foundations.* Boston: Houghton Mifflin.

King, M. (1988). *Ordinary Olympians.* Transforming Education (IC #18). Winter. Pg. 14.

Kohn, A. (2008). *Progressive education: why it's hard to beat, but also hard to find.* Independent School Magazine. Spring.

Kozol, J. (1992). *Savage Inequalities: Children in America's Schools.* New York: Harper Perennial.

Lakin, R. (2007). *Teaching as an Act of Love: Thoughts and Recollections of a Former Teacher, Principal and Kid.* Bloomington: iUniverse.

McGhan, B. (2002). March. *A fundamental education reform: Teacher-led schools.* Phi Delta Kappan.

Morrison, G.S. (2009). *Child-centered education today.* Early Childhood Education. NY: Merrill.

Moustafa, M. (1997). *Beyond Traditional Phonics.* **Portsmouth, NH: Heinemann.**

Neve, C. D., Hart, L., and Thomas, E. (1986). October. Huge learning jumps show potency of brain-based instruction. *Kappan.*

Noddings, N. (2005). The Challenge to Care in Schools. NY: Teachers College Press.

Noddings, N. (2003). Happiness and Education. NY: Cambridge University Press.

Odiorne, G. (1974). *Management and the activity trap.* New York: Harper & Row.

O'Hanian, S. (1999). *One Size Fits Few: The Folly of Educational Standards.* **Portsmouth, NH: Heinemann.**

Park, G., Lubinski, D., and Benbow, C.P. (2008). *When childhood collides with NCLB.* **The Vermont Society for the Study of Education, Brandon, VT.**

Pearsall, P. (2003). *The Heart's Code: Tapping the Wisdom and Power of Our Heart Energy.* NY: Broadway Books. and "The Thinking Heart" an interview with Paul Pearsall. Hal Bennett and Susan Sparrow.

Postman, N. and Weingartner, C. (1969). *Teaching as a Subversive Activity.* New York: Dell.

Posner, R. (2009). Lives of Passion, School of Hope. Boulder, CO: Sentient Publications.

Prensky, M., (2008). *Young minds, fast times.* Edutopia. 4(3), 33-36.

Rogers, C. (1966). To facilitate learning. In *Innovations for time to teach.* Washington, DC: National Education Association.

Schwartz, J., and Begley, S. (2002). *The mind and the brain: Neuroplasticity and the power of mental force.* New York: Harper Collins.

Smith, F. (1986). *Understanding Reading,* **3rd. ed. Mahwah, NJ: Lawrence Erlbaum Associates.**

Smith, F. (2003). *Unspeakable Acts, Unnatural Practices: Flaws and Fallacies in "Scientific" Reading Instruction.* N.H.: Heinemann

Schwahn, C. and Spady, W. (2010). *Total Leaders 2.0: Leading in the Age of Empowerment.* MD: Rowman & Littlefield Education.

Schwahn, C. and Spady, W. (2010). *Learning Communities 2.0: Educating in the Age of Empowerment.* MD: Rowman & Littlefield Education.

Spady, W. (2007). *The Paradigm Trap: Getting Beyond the No Child Left Behind Policy,* Education Week 26 (18), 27-29.

Spring, J. (2007). *American Education.* New York: McGraw-Hill.

Stigler, J, and Hiebert, J. (1999). *The Teaching Gap.* New York: Free Press/Simon and Schuster, Inc.

Stoddard, L. (1992). *Redesigning education: A guide for developing human greatness.* Tucson, AZ: Zephyr Press.

Stoddard, L. (2009). *Educating for Human Greatness, CD Version, First Edition.* Brandon, VT: Holistic Education Press.

Taylor, C. W. (1990). *Expanded awareness of creative potentials worldwide.* Salt Lake City: Brain Talent Powers Press.

Thomas, F. (1982). The Liberty of the Citizen. *The Granada Guildhall Lectures.* Granada.

Williams, R. (1967). *You Are Extraordinary.* NewYork: Random House.

Williamson, M. A. (1992). Return to Love: Reflections on the Principles of A Course in Miracles. Chapter 7, Section 3. NY: Harper Collins.

Williamson, P., B. E. Langley, L., and Dina, M. (2005). *Meeting the challenge of high-stakes testing while remaining child-centered.* Childhood Education: Summer.

* High priority reading is in bold type.

Educating for Human Greatness
We offer discounts for orders of 10 or more.

See our website for details and downloadable order form
or to pay by credit card.

Mailing Address for Orders: We Invoice Purchase Orders!

EfHG
Dr. Anthony Dallmann-Jones
440 Seaview Court - Suite 1911
Marco Island, Florida 34145

Call our offices to discuss:
Educating for Human Greatness
Keynotes, Seminars and Workshops

EfHG National Office Contact Information:

Tel: 920-251-2052
Fax: 888-678-4902

Email: asdjones@gmail.com
Official EfHG website: www.EfHG.org

Call or email if you wish to book
Lynn or Tony to speak or consult!

CPSIA information can be obtained
at www.ICGtesting.com
Printed in the USA
LVOW08s1842180617
538521LV00001B/105/P